Drama Techniques
Third Edition

Cambridge Handbooks for Language Teachers

This is a series of practical guides for teachers of English and other languages. Illustrative examples are usually drawn from the field of English as a foreign or second language, but the ideas and techniques described can equally well be used in the teaching of any language.

Recent titles in this series:

Ways of Doing
Students explore their everyday and classroom processes
PAUL DAVIS, BARBARA GARSIDE *and*
MARIO RINVOLUCRI

Using Newspapers in the Classroom
PAUL SANDERSON

Teaching Adult Second Language Learners
HEATHER MCKAY *and* ABIGAIL TOM

Teaching English Spelling
A practical guide
RUTH SHEMESH *and* SHEILA WALLER

Using Folktales
ERIC TAYLOR

Personalizing Language Learning
Personalized language learning activities
GRIFF GRIFFITHS *and* KATHRYN KEOHANE

Teach Business English
A comprehensive introduction to Business English
SYLVIE DONNA

Learner Autonomy
A guide to activities which encourage learner responsibility
ÁGOTA SCHARLE *and* ANITA SZABÓ

The Internet and the Language Classroom
Practical classroom activities and projects
GAVIN DUDENEY

Planning Lessons and Courses
Designing sequences of work for the language classroom
TESSA WOODWARD

Using the Board in the Language Classroom
JEANNINE DOBBS

Learner English (second edition)
MICHAEL SWAN *and* BERNARD SMITH

Teaching Large Multilevel Classes
NATALIE HESS

Writing Simple Poems
Pattern poetry for language acquisition
VICKI L. HOLMES *and* MARGARET R. MOULTON

Laughing Matters
Humour in the language classroom
PÉTER MEDGYES

Using Authentic Video in the Language Classroom
JANE SHERMAN

Stories
Narrative activities for the language classroom
RUTH WAJNRYB

Language Activities for Teenagers
edited by SETH LINDSTROMBERG

Pronunciation Practice Activities
A resource book for teaching English pronunciation
MARTIN HEWINGS

Five-Minute Activities for Business English
PAUL EMMERSON *and* NICK HAMILTON

Drama Techniques
Third Edition

A resource book of communication activities for language teachers

Alan Maley and Alan Duff

Consultant and editor: Penny Ur

CAMBRIDGE
UNIVERSITY PRESS

CAMBRIDGE UNIVERSITY PRESS
Cambridge, New York, Melbourne, Madrid, Cape Town, Singapore, São Paulo

Cambridge University Press
The Edinburgh Building, Cambridge CB2 2RU, UK

www.cambridge.org
Information on this title: www.cambridge.org/9780521601191

First published 1978
Second edition 1982
Third edition 2005
2nd printing 2006

Printed in the United Kingdom at the University Press, Cambridge

A catalogue record for this publication is available from the British Library

ISBN-13 978-0-521-60119-1 paperback
ISBN-10 0-521-60119-3 paperback

Contents

Thanks and acknowledgements   x
Introduction   1

1 **Getting ready**   6
    Non-verbal warming-up activities   7
1.1   Handshakes   7
1.2   Hand catching   8
1.3   Mirror hands   9
1.4   Numbers in your head   11
1.5   Clap around the circle   12
1.6   Swings   13
1.7   Catch the ball   15
1.8   Beat out that rhythm   16
1.9   Touch it   17
1.10   Blind   17
    Non-verbal cooling-down activities   18
1.11   Breathing   18
1.12   Feeling my space   19
1.13   Feeling your muscles   20
1.14   From seed to plant   21
1.15   Slow motion   21
1.16   Just relax   22
1.17   Directed relaxation   23
1.18   Going with the flow   24
    Verbal exercises   26
1.19   Football wave   26
1.20   Can you do this?   27
1.21   The sun and the moon   27
1.22   Back writing   28
1.23   Gobbledy-gook   29
1.24   And I'm a butcher   30
1.25   Let me tell you something about X   30
1.26   Something in common   31
1.27   Directed group visualisation   32

Contents

1.28 Childhood memories 33
1.29 Personalities/celebrities 34
Group formation activities 35
1.30 Strings 35
1.31 Atom 3! 36
1.32 Mix and mingle 36
1.33 I've got my eye on you! 36
1.34 I know what I like 37

2 **Observation** 38
2.1 Freeze! 38
2.2 Back-to-back 39
2.3 Say 'Cheese' 40
2.4 Just listening 40
2.5 I said, he said, she said … 41
2.6 Minimal differences 42
2.7 My potato 43
2.8 Kim's game 44
2.9 Familiar scenes 45
2.10 Like me? Like you? 46
2.11 First this, then that … 47
2.12 Picture memory 48

3 **Working with mime** 50
3.1 What am I doing? 50
3.2 My word 53
3.3 Metronome mime 54
3.4 Difficulty with large or small objects 55
3.5 Exchanging objects 56
3.6 Taste, touch, smell … 57
3.7 What time of day is it? 59
3.8 Mimes from the past 60
3.9 Miming a poem 61
3.10 Miming noises 63
3.11 Normal, slow, fast 64
3.12 Hotel receptionist 66

4 **Working with the voice** 69
Preparing for voicework 69
4.1 Relaxation 70
4.2 Physical warm ups 71

4.3	Breathing	73
4.4	Warming up the voice	75
4.5	Preparing the articulators	77
4.6	Volume	78
	Working with the voice	79
4.7	Thinking about my voice	79
4.8	Changing voices	81
4.9	Delayed repetition	83
4.10	Working on words	84
4.11	A vocal tapestry	85
4.12	Shifting the stress	87
4.13	Listing	88
4.14	Elastic sentences	89
4.15	Playing with the text	92
4.16	Listen to me!	95
4.17	Group orchestration of texts	96
5	**Working with objects**	99
5.1	What am I holding?	99
5.2	My special object, your special object ...	101
5.3	Metamorphosis	102
5.4	The envelope	103
5.5	The all-purpose object	104
5.6	Stone, wood and metal	105
5.7	It meant a lot to me ...	107
5.8	Fashion show	107
5.9	Where did you get that hat?	108
5.10	Masks	110
5.11	What am I bid?	111
5.12	Symbols and icons	113
5.13	Who's the owner?	114
6	**Working with visuals**	116
6.1	Self-portraits	116
6.2	Identikit	118
6.3	From my album	119
6.4	Space invaders	120
6.5	High points	123
6.6	Portraits	124
6.7	Becoming a picture	126

Contents

6.8   Bringing a picture to life   127

6.9   Picture sets   129

6.10   Faces and places   130

6.11   Split cartoons   131

6.12   Mood pictures   135

6.13   Pictures from music   136

6.14   Recreating the scene   138

6.15   Guided visualisation   139

6.16   Characters from fiction   142

7   Working with the imagination   145

7.1   Something in common   145

7.2   Statues   146

7.3   Amazimbi   147

7.4   Patent pending   149

7.5   Making a machine   150

7.6   Waking dream   152

7.7   Festival   153

7.8   It's against the law   154

7.9   Time's arrow   156

7.10   Our new constitution   157

8   Working from/into words, phrases, sentences   160

8.1   My favourite word   160

8.2   The feel of words   161

8.3   Real English or not?   163

8.4   What's in a name?   165

8.5   Words and movement   166

8.6   Tableaux   168

8.7   Praise songs   169

8.8   Group story   170

8.9   Off the cuff   171

8.10   Mirror words   172

8.11   Charades   174

8.12   Split headlines   175

8.13   Split exchanges   177

8.14   People, places, problems and things   180

8.15   Odd news   182

8.16   Proverbs in action   184

8.17   First lines   186

9 **Working from/into texts** 189
9.1 Mini-texts 189
9.2 What next? 192
9.3 Starters 194
9.4 Tops and tails 196
9.5 Jumbled stories 198
9.6 What are they saying? 200
9.7 Stop press 202

10 **Working from/into scenarios and scripts** 205
10.1 One-word dialogues 205
10.2 Dialogue interpretation 207
10.3 Alibi 209
10.4 Just a minute 210
10.5 Telephone conversations 213
10.6 Conflict 216
10.7 Tension 218
10.8 The hole 220
10.9 Role reversal 222
10.10 A real bargain 224
10.11 Real theatre scripts 226

11 **Into Performance** 229
Benefits from performance 229
How to tackle the 'Play project' 230
Selecting a play 230
Getting to know the text 232
Warming up 234
Improvisation 234
Rehearsal 235
Involving everyone 237
A few practical considerations 238
Some possible sources for plays 239

Bibliography 240

Index 244

Acknowledgements

This book is dedicated to all those students, teachers, trainers, colleagues and friends who have used the earlier editions with such enthusiasm. Their ideas and feedback have formed a valued part of the input into this new edition, and their professional support has given us the inspiration to complete it. We are most grateful to Penny Ur for her wise and practical suggestions in the formative stage, and to Yvonne Harmer and Frances Amrani for their care in editing the final manuscript.

The authors and publishers are grateful to the following for permission to reproduce copyright material. It has not been possible to identify the sources of all the material used and in such cases the publishers would welcome information from copyright owners.

Text: P. 94 'Notice' by Elma Mitchell, Peterloo Poets Cornwall; p. 97 'We know' from *Wicked World* by Benjamin Zephaniah (Puffin, 2000) Text copyright © Benjamin Zephaniah, 2000; p. 98 'Once Upon a Time' by John Agard; p. 122 'The First Men on Mercury' in *Collected Poems* by Edwin Morgan 1982 by permission of Carcanet Press Limited; p. 143 *The Blue Film* by Graham Greene; *When Greek meets Greek* by Graham Greene, *The Basement Room* by Graham Greene, *Jubilee* by Graham Greene by kind permission of David Higham Associates, London; p. 191 *Thinking in English* by Leszek Szkutnik, Poland; p. 192 'The Mother' by Anne Stevenson, from *The Collected Poems* (OUP, 1996; Bloodaxe Books, 2000); p. 193 'The Lovers' from *Poems* by W R Rodgers 1941 by kind permission of the Estate of W.R.Rodgers and the Gallery Press, Loughcrew, Oldcastle, County Meath, Ireland; p. 193 'The Inner Man' by Christine M Banks Copyright © Telegraph Group Limited and contributors; p. 195 'The Voice' by V.S. Pritchett; 'My Beloved Charioteer' by Shashi Deshpande; p. 195–6 *The Snows of Kilimanjaro* by Ernest Hemingway; p. 196 *Pictures* by Katherine Mansfield; p. 197 'A Bee Life' from *Tragically I was an only twin* by Peter Cook published by Random House by kind permission of David Higham Associates, London; p. 204 'Lifeboat Crew Rescue' by Ian Read in the *Canterbury Christmas Special* 26th December 2003 published by Kent Regional Newspapers; p. 212 'To M.M.' by Gerald England; p. 212 'Take a Pew' by Alan Bennett by kind permission of PFD, London; p. 215 'Bingo' by Edward Bond; p. 227 'The Dumb Waiter' by Harold Pinter in *The Birthday Party and Other Plays* by kind permission of Faber and Faber Ltd., London.

Photos: P. 118 advertisement photos Rank Xerox (UK) Ltd; p. 125 *Bertrand Russell* reproduced by permission Corbis, London; p. 128 *Masons of the Mall* by Beryl Cook © 2000 taken from the Bumper Edition, Victor Gollancz, London. Reproduced by permission of Rogers, Coleridge & White, London; p. 132–4 Jean-Jacques Sempé; p. 136 Renoir: *Dancing at the Moulin de la Galette* reproduced by permission Corbis, London; p. 139 Pryanshinikov, Illarion Mikhailovich: *Before the Wedding* reproduced by permission of the Bridgeman Art Library, London

The publisher has used its best endeavours to ensure that the URLs for external websites referred to in this book are correct and active at the time of going to press. However, the publisher has no responsibility for the websites and can make no guarantee that a site will remain live or that the content is or will remain appropriate.

Introduction

This is the third edition of *Drama Techniques in Language Teaching*. The second edition has been going strong for over 20 years. We are confident that this, the third edition, will be equally popular with teachers world-wide.

The kinds of techniques or activities we advocated in the earlier editions are now well accepted by many teachers, though they were pioneering stuff at the time. Things have moved on, however, and we felt it was time for a completely new edition which would cut out some less useful activities, revamp others and introduce completely new material and ideas.

Why use drama?

- It integrates language skills in a natural way. Careful listening is a key feature. Spontaneous verbal expression is integral to most of the activities; and many of them require reading and writing, both as part of the input and the output.
- It integrates verbal and non-verbal aspects of communication, thus bringing together both mind and body, and restoring the balance between physical and intellectual aspects of learning.
- It draws upon both cognitive and affective domains, thus restoring the importance of feeling as well as thinking.
- By fully contextualising the language, it brings the classroom interaction to life through an intense focus on meaning.
- The emphasis on whole-person learning and multi-sensory inputs helps learners to capitalise on their strengths and to extend their range. In doing so, it offers unequalled opportunities for catering to learner differences.
- It fosters self-awareness (and awareness of others), self-esteem and confidence; and through this, motivation is developed.
- Motivation is likewise fostered and sustained through the variety and sense of expectancy generated by the activities.
- There is a transfer of responsibility for learning from teacher to learners – which is where it belongs.

- It encourages an open, exploratory style of learning where creativity and the imagination are given scope to develop. This, in turn, promotes risk-taking, which is an essential element in effective language learning.
- It has a positive effect on classroom dynamics and atmosphere, thus facilitating the formation of a bonded group, which learns together.
- It is an enjoyable experience.
- It is low-resource. For most of the time, all you need is a 'roomful of human beings'.

What are drama techniques?

They are activities, many of which are based on techniques used by actors in their training. Through them, students are given opportunities to use their own personality in creating the material on which part of the language class is based. They draw on the natural ability of everyone to imitate, mimic and express themselves through gesture and facial expression. They draw, too, on students' imagination and memory, and their natural capacity to bring to life parts of their past experience that might never otherwise emerge. They are dramatic because they arouse our interest, which they do in part by drawing upon the unpredictable power generated when one person is brought together with others. Every student brings a different life, a different background, a different set of memories and associations into the class. It is this we seek to tap into; and in doing so, we inevitably restore some of the neglected emotional content to language, along with a renewed attention to what is physical about language.

Some practical points

These comments apply to the standard format for activities in this series: *Aims, Focus, Level, Time, Preparation, Procedure, Follow-on, Variation(s)* and *Note(s)*.

- *Aim* This indicates the broad reasons for doing the activity.
- *Focus* This relates to the narrower, linguistic objectives. These are sometimes expressed in terms of syntax, lexis or phonology; sometimes in terms of language functions; and sometimes in terms of spoken discourse over longer stretches of language. It is important to remember that, in drama work, it is not possible totally to predict what language features will occur, so the focus can only be indicative of what we think will happen; it cannot predict what will happen.

- *Level* The important thing to remember here is that the same activity can often be done at many different levels, drawing on whatever language the students my be able to use. Even in cases where we have prescribed an activity for Elementary, for instance, it may well be possible to exploit it at Advanced level, too.
- *Time* Similarly, it is difficult to set accurate timings. Many of the timings are based on the assumption that you will be using an activity for a whole class hour, so we need to give some guidance on how much time should be devoted to each stage. But sometimes, you may feel an activity is going so well that you want to let it run. Ultimately, it is up to you to exercise your professional judgement based on your intuition.
- *Preparation* Most of the activities require little or no special equipment or material. All you really need is a 'roomful of human beings'. Nonetheless, you still sometimes need some basic materials for the activity, such as cards, OHTs, objects or pictures. Sometimes you will also need to ask students to bring materials or objects to class.
- *Procedure* This specifies the steps you should go through to implement the activity. You may need to be flexible here too. With large classes, you may need to vary group size. With small classes, the group is already very small, so you may need to vary the instructions accordingly.
- *Follow-on* This suggests ways in which the activity can be extended, either in class or as homework.
- *Variation(s)* This suggests alternative ways of doing the activity, or slightly different yet related activities.
- *Note(s)* This provides comments on the activity. Some activities include reference to other published sources.

Some important points to bear in mind

The importance of discussion
Many, if not most of these activities require students to work in pairs or groups to reach agreement on how they will conduct their work and how they will present the outcome. This is an essential part of the activity. There is no point in rushing into an activity for its own sake. The quality of the product, both linguistic and dramatic, depends largely on the quality of the preparatory discussion.

Use of the mother tongue
There is a growing climate of opinion in favour of judicious and selective use of the mother tongue in foreign-language classes. Clearly, if taken to

extremes, this can transform the foreign-language class into a mother-tongue class, which would be counterproductive and nonsensical. For drama work, it may be sensible at first to allow a limited use of the mother tongue in discussion (indeed it may be impossible to prevent it), while insisting on the use of English in the actual activity. As time goes by, however, and students become more familiar with the English expressions needed for discussion, they should be encouraged progressively to use more English.

Re-cycling of known language

We need to remember that the primary function of drama techniques is to offer opportunities for use of language already learnt. It is not primarily to teach new items. This does not, of course, preclude a good deal of incidental learning, whether from teacher input (supplying a missing phrase or word) or from peers (the class as a group has much greater linguistic resources than the individuals who make it up).

The teacher's role

Remember that you do not need to be a trained drama expert in order to introduce drama into your teaching, though some training, especially of the voice, is desirable. For drama activities to work well, teachers themselves need to be convinced that they will work. A class rapidly senses any hesitancy or nervousness, or lack of conviction on the part of the teacher. You are the key to the success of these activities. If you do them reluctantly, or half-heartedly, it is better not to do them at all.

How to do it

How will you convey this commitment? You will show your confidence through your 'open' body language, by the firm yet friendly tone of your voice, by demonstrating that you know what you are doing through being well prepared and organised, by giving helpful, non-threatening feedback, by being good humoured: in short, by creating an atmosphere of relaxed energy in which everyone can experience the 'flow' experience. Does this sound like you? If it does, then we hope you will enjoy using this book, and continue to extend your range as a teacher. If it does not – why not give it a try anyway? Many teachers who started out using drama techniques with some trepidation report that the experience has changed their lives.

So, what's new?

The third edition is a radical revision of the second edition. The main changes are:

- Most of the activities are now in the new series format, and have been completely rewritten.
- We have cut a large number of activities which experience has shown to be less useful.
- We have added a large number of new activities.
- We have completely reorganised the structure of the book, reordering activities, and adding new chapters on Voice and Performance.

In short, this is a *new* book, even though it draws substantially on the ideas and materials from the earlier edition. We hope you will enjoy using it.

1   Getting ready

This chapter includes both non-verbal and verbal activities. None of them take very long to do. All of them are intended to get students in the mood for more extended drama activities. More specifically:

- They all involve a degree of physical activity, thus helping to restore the balance between thinking and doing.
- They help put students in a relaxed, less inhibited state, in which they are more receptive than they might otherwise be. This helps to lower the threshold of unconscious resistance to learning a foreign language, and to foster more open, creative work in subsequent activities.
- They help to develop confidence and cooperation with others. Being aware of others and how we relate to them is an important aspect of class bonding.
- They can help students to make a smooth transition from their activities outside the class (perhaps a lesson in a different subject, or the stress of coming from a job in heavy traffic) to the learning atmosphere of the language class.
- They may also be used to make smooth links between one activity and the next.

There are four main types of activity:

1 non-verbal warming up
2 non-verbal relaxation / cooling down
3 activities involving language
4 group formation activities.

The way you choose to use the activities is up to you. As you come to get the feel of your class group, you will know best which ones to use at which moments. There is no grading, though activities are presented in clusters when they share common elements.

There are a number of further general points to be made:

1 Most of these activities involve physical activity. You will need to be vigilant to ensure that things do not get out of hand, and that students observe care and attention for others.

2 Some of the activities recommend lying on the floor. This must be at your discretion. If there is insufficient space, or if surfaces are too hard or dirty, students can usually do the activity standing or sitting.

3 Many activities involve physical contact between students. In some societies, such contact is taboo. Make sure that it is acceptable before launching into it. (Note that it is often possible to do these activities if males are paired with males, and females with females.)

4 Many of the activities are good ways of warming up a group of students who do not yet know each other. It is important therefore that they change partners as often as possible so as to interact with a larger number of other students.

5 For many of the activities you may need to demonstrate the procedure with one of the students.

Non–verbal warming-up activities

1.1 Handshakes

Aim	To have everyone in the group meet and have contact with everyone else
Level	All
Time	5–10 minutes

Procedure

1 Clear space in the room so that students can walk around freely.
2 Tell students to walk around the room. As they do so, they should shake hands with every other member of the group as they meet them. Each time they shake hands, they should make eye contact with the other person and hold it for a few seconds, and smile.

Variations

1 Students mill around in the space. As they do so, they must try to meet as many other students as possible. When they meet, they should shake hands, smile and say: *I'm (name). Nice to meet you.*
Repeat the activity. This time, they say: *Hello (name of the other person). Nice to see you again. How are things?* Obviously, you can vary the phrases they say to each other.

2 If students have trouble recalling names, the person being greeted should help them out. You can also teach the ploy: *Hello. Nice to meet you again. Now you are ...* (hesitation when the other person will usually

supply his/her name!) as well as some useful face-saving expressions, such as: *I'm very good at faces but I'm terrible with names*, etc.

3 You may wish to set the occasion for the greeting. For example: a reunion party for school friends who have not met for ten years; a wedding bringing together family members who have not met since the last wedding ten years ago; a funeral gathering of an ex-colleague, etc. Alternatively, give students a theme word, such as *Cheerful*, *Sad*, *Disappointed*, *Hurry*. They then shake hands in a way that reflects the theme word. Change the theme word several times.

1.2 Hand catching

Aim To release some of the nervous energy students often bring with them to class – this helps prepare them for more sustained activities
Level All
Time 5–10 minutes

Procedure

1 Students stand in pairs facing each other. One partner holds out both hands, palms facing inwards, about 25 cm apart (see illustration).

2 The other partner tries to quickly pass his/her right hand vertically between the partner's hands without getting caught in the trap, which can close at any time.

3   Reverse roles: the one caught becomes the catcher. After a few turns, change partners.

Variations

1   Student 1 holds out two hands palms down. Student 2 places hands, palms facing up, underneath. Student 1 tries to catch one of Student 2's palms by a quick slap down. Student 2 tries to move before getting slapped.
2   Students face each other in pairs with their left hands behind their backs, palms facing outward. When you say *Go*, each student tries to touch their partner's left palm with their right hand while avoiding being touched themselves. After a couple of minutes, change partners. Continue changing partners every few minutes.

1.3 Mirror hands

Aim	To develop concentration and anticipation of what a partner will do next
Level	All
Time	10 minutes

Procedure

1   Students stand in pairs facing each other with their hands raised to shoulder height, palms facing outward, and as close to their partner's hands as possible *without* actually touching (see illustration).

2   One student is the 'leader' and begins to move both hands in a plane, i.e. always keeping the palms facing toward the partner's hands. The partner must try to follow the movements as accurately as possible, as if in a mirror.
3   After a few minutes, the other partner takes the role of 'leader'.

Variation

Students face each other in pairs with hands raised to shoulder height and palms touching their partner's palms (see illustration). They move their hands slowly in as many different directions as possible without losing palm contact. After a few minutes, pairs become threes and continue the movements. A few minutes later, threes become fours and continue.

Notes

1   The need to concentrate on another person is analogous to the sort of anticipation demanded in verbal exchanges. It also develops a high degree of eye contact between partners.
2   You may suggest to students that they use the whole space available, i.e. from high above the head to the feet, and from side to side.
3   You may also need to remind them that this is a cooperative, not a competitive, activity!

1.4 Numbers in your head

Aim	To give physical shape to numbers in a foreign language
Focus	Cardinal numbers
Level	All
Time	10 minutes

Procedure

1 Each student finds a space to stand in. With eyes closed, everyone traces the shapes of the numbers from 0 to 9 simply by moving their heads only (no movement of the trunk, etc.) to follow the shapes. As they trace each number, they 'say' the number silently (in the foreign language!) in their heads.

2 Then ask one student to call out numbers at random, e.g. 51, 93, 66, etc. The other students keep eyes closed and make the shapes of the numbers with their heads as they are called out.

3 In pairs, facing each other with eyes open, one partner makes a number with the head, the other guesses what it is.

Variations

1 Ask students to make the letters of the alphabet in this way too.

2 Students find a place to stand where they can extend their arms fully without touching anyone else. One student is chosen to call out numbers between 0 and 9. As each number is called, the other students try to form its shape using their whole bodies. They hold the shape until the next number is called.

3 In groups of seven or eight, students decide on a word with the same number of letters as the number of group members (e.g. for a group of seven, *bananas* would fit). Each student then becomes one letter of the word. They have to form the shape of the letter with their whole body. Each group then presents its word to the others, who try to guess what it is.

4 In pairs, students take turns to use their index finger to trace in the air the shape of a number from 0 to 9. The partner guesses the number being traced. Students then change partners and move on to the letters of the alphabet, and to writing two- and three-digit numbers for each other to 'read'. Finally, they write simple words in the air for their new partner to interpret.

Notes

1 Numbers are notoriously difficult to master in a foreign language. By reinforcing the number shape using body movement, the activity helps students to apprehend numbers in a more profound way and to integrate them physically. They feel as well as see and hear the numbers. By presenting the numbers in an unfamiliar way, involving the kinaesthetic dimension, the numbers and letters are reinforced through another modality.

2 Speaking the numbers silently is also important for reinforcement.

3 The activity gives excellent exercise to the neck and throat muscles, so important in producing speech!

1.5 Clap around the circle

Aims	To develop quick reactions; to facilitate non-verbal contact between students
Level	All
Time	10–15 minutes

Procedure

1 Students stand in a big circle, if possible leaving about one metre between each student.

2 The teacher chooses one student to start. This student turns towards the next student on the right and claps hands towards that student, as if throwing the clap for them to catch.

3 The student 'catches' the clap by clapping, then turns to the right and claps to the next student, who also catches this clap, turns to the right and throws a clap to the next student … and so on, all round the circle.

Variations

1 When the clap returns to the student who started, reverse the direction, i.e. to the left.

2 Choose two students on opposite sides of the circle. One will send the clap to the right, the other to the left. Students need to be very alert, especially when the two claps cross over!

3 Choose one student to start. They clap towards any other student in the circle. This student claps as they receive it, then sends it to any other student in the circle. The clapping messages criss-cross the circle.

4 As in 3, but students add a short message as they clap. For example: A *Here you are.* B *Thanks a lot.*

5 Instead of clapping, students throw an imaginary ball, object or small animal to each other. Each time a student receives something they must transform it into something else before throwing it on.

Notes

1 This is a lively activity which keeps students alert and on their toes.
2 You will need to make sure students both catch and throw their claps – so each student claps twice each time. Try to get a fast pace going.
3 With a very large class, students can form several circles, depending on space available.

See also 1.7 Catch the ball.

1.6 Swings

Aims	To develop mutual trust and confidence among students; to develop group cooperation; to help students relax before more demanding activities
Levels	All
Time	5–10 minutes

Procedure

1 Students form groups of eight.
2 Seven students form the swing (see illustration): three on each side and one to support the head of the eighth.

3 The eighth student lies on the swing formed by the other students. They then slowly and gently swing the reclining student backwards and forwards a few times.

4 Everyone has a turn in the swing.

Variations

1 In pairs, one student stands behind the other. The student in front falls backwards, and is caught by the student behind (see illustration). Students alternate several times as 'fallers' and 'catchers'. They then do the activity again, this time facing each other.

2 Students form threes. The student falling stands between the other two and falls first backwards, then forwards. Each time, the catching student will gently push the falling student upright again. Take care, especially with teenagers!

3 Students work in groups of about eight. They form a circle. One student stands in the middle of each circle. This student folds arms and closes eyes. The other students stand about 30 cm away from him or her, and raise their hands to about shoulder height, with palms facing outward. The student in the middle then falls in any direction. The others must gently stop him or her falling, and gently push him or her in another direction (see illustration).

Notes

1 This is a very relaxing and enjoyable activity requiring considerable coordination and cooperation between students.

2 Make sure students understand the importance of doing the activity gently! For this reason, it may be an activity you would not do with teenagers! It is also best done on a carpeted floor, though this is not essential provided due care is taken not to drop the swinger!

3 The activity (and the Variations) is important for developing both self-confidence and mutual confidence; both of these are important qualities for drama work. Some students will be afraid of letting themselves fall. Gradually, however, if you do the activity more than once, they will develop the self-confidence to let themselves go.

1.7 Catch the ball

Aims	To develop physical anticipation, cooperation and rapport
Level	All
Time	5–10 minutes

Procedure

1 Students work in pairs. They stand opposite each other and throw and catch an imaginary (invisible) ball to and fro between them.

2 After a few minutes, change partners.

Variations

1 Students stand in two lines of equal length, facing each other. The ball is then thrown by one student on one side to any student on the other.
2 In pairs, students play an imaginary game of table tennis.

Notes

1 Explain that it is important for students to really 'feel' and 'see' the ball – its size, weight, texture, etc. To help them do this, suggest the type of ball they are throwing: football, balloon (very light), tennis ball, ping-pong ball, medicine ball (very heavy), etc. If done well, it should almost be possible for an observer to 'see' the ball as it moves between them.
2 The activity is good preparation for some of the activities in chapter 3 (Working with mime).

See also 1.5 Clap around the circle.

1.8 Beat out that rhythm

Aim	To encourage disciplined cooperation by learning to fit in with and respond to others' physical actions
Level	All
Time	10–15 minutes

Procedure

1 Students work in groups of about ten. They should sit in a circle, preferably on the floor.
2 Designate one student to begin beating out a simple, not too fast, regular rhythm on the floor (or by clapping hands, clicking fingers, tapping a chair with a pen, etc.).
3 Once the rhythm is well established, the next student to the right adds in a variation to the main rhythm. Then the next student to the right adds another element, and so on, until a composite beat results.
4 If there is more than one group, let each group perform its rhythms for the others.

Variations

1 When a group has more or less finalised its 'performance', they may wish to polish it up, for example by varying volume – starting off very soft, working up to a climax and fading away at the end.
2 The groups may like to add words to their performance in the form of a simple chant which will fit the main rhythm.

Note

This activity requires a lot of self-discipline and concentration; students need to tune their contributions so that they do not drown out those of others. They also need to hold on to their own beat in spite of all the other sounds going on around them.

See also 4.11 A vocal tapestry.

1.9 Touch it

Aims	To encourage observation of the classroom environment; to make sure students mix freely with each other in a friendly atmosphere
Level	All
Time	5–10 minutes

Procedure
1 Students form a group in the middle of the room.
2 The teacher then calls out a number of objects, surfaces, colours, textures, etc. in turn, e.g. *Touch something smooth. Touch something red*, etc. Students carry out the instructions as quickly as possible.

Variation

With more advanced students, the instructions can be made correspondingly more demanding (e.g. *Touch something with a corrugated surface. Find something used for perforating paper*, etc.).

Note

A very good mixing activity, which can also involve some vocabulary reinforcement.

1.10 Blind

Aim	To develop confidence, trust and mutual consideration between members of a group
Level	All
Time	10 minutes
Preparation	Bring in suitable items to act as blindfolds (optional); you will need to rearrange the classroom furniture to make a kind of obstacle course.

Procedure

1 Students choose a partner, and decide who will be the blind person and who the guide. Blind people either bind their eyes with a blindfold or close their eyes tightly (no cheating, please!).

2 The guides then take their blind partner by the arm, and silently and gently guide them around the room, taking care to avoid banging into any objects on the way.

3 Partners then change roles and repeat the process. If there is time, repeat the activity with a different partner.

4 If there is time, discuss briefly how students felt, both as guide and as blind person.

Note
In a large class, it may be better to limit the numbers of pairs operating at one time, to avoid collisions.

See also Chapter 11, *Warming up*.

Non-verbal cooling-down activities

1.11 Breathing

Aims	To help students control their breathing; to develop concentration and a sense of calm
Level	All
Time	10 minutes

Procedure

1 Students find a space to stand in, then stand erect with their eyes closed.

2 On your word, students breathe in deeply, then release the breath slowly and evenly.

3 Students continue to do this for ten breaths. Each time, they should hold the air longer before releasing it. They should also try to release the air more slowly each time. You can help them by counting aloud for them: *In – two, three, four. Hold – two, three, four. Out – two, three, four; In – two, three, four, five*, etc.

4 Then ask students to sing a given note (*Aaaaah, Uuuuu, Oooooh*, etc.) as they exhale. Repeat this several times.

Variations

1 Work as in step 4, but this time students start the note very loud and gradually let it fade away on the out breath.
2 Students form two equally-sized groups. On the out breath, one group starts the note very loud and fades away; the other group starts very soft and ends very loud.

Notes

1 This may seem like a trivial activity, but breath is the source of the spoken word. Many people breathe in a very shallow manner, and therefore have insufficient air to sustain their speech. This activity focuses attention on breathing and its effects.
2 Deep breathing has a calming effect and helps concentration. Tell students it is one thing many great actors do to centre themselves just before they go on stage.
3 Keeping eyes closed may seem a bit strange, but it does help concentration.

See also 4.3 Breathing.

1.12 Feeling my space

Aims	To raise awareness of the body and the way it fits into its environment; to relax in preparation for another activity
Level	All
Time	5–10 minutes

Procedure

1 Students lie comfortably on their backs on the floor, with eyes closed. Leave enough space between students to allow them to extend their limbs in all directions without invading anyone else's space.
2 Tell students to stretch out their bodies as far as possible, expanding to occupy all their space.
3 Students hold this position for a few seconds. Then tell them to contract back into the smallest space possible. They hold this position too.
4 Repeat the process several times. Then let students lie quietly for a few seconds before getting up.

Notes

1 Give your instructions in a calm yet firm voice. The quality of your voice is an important ingredient in making students feel relaxed.

2 If there is not enough space to lie down, students can still do the activity sitting in chairs, though this is less satisfactory.

See also 4.1 Relaxation, 4.2 Physical warm ups.

1.13 Feeling your muscles

Aims	To develop body awareness and control of muscles all over the body; to relax in preparation for other activities
Level	All
Time	10 minutes

Procedure
1 Students lie comfortably on the floor in their own space, with eyes closed.
2 When you give the instruction, students tense *all* their muscles and hold them tense until told to relax again.
3 Repeat this several times. Then let students lie quietly for a moment before they get up.

Variation
Students lie down and are told to go completely 'floppy'. You need to check this by walking round and picking up arms or legs to see if there is any muscular tension. Next, students are told to start tensing muscles one after the other, starting with the toes and working gradually upwards until the whole body is tensed. Then students relax the muscles progressively from head back to the toes. Again, let students lie relaxed for a moment before getting up.

Notes
1 Like breathing, the way we use our muscles is also habitual. We tend to rely on a rather restricted range of muscles and to forget about the others. This activity helps redirect conscious attention to all our muscles. Language is physical and involves using parts of our bodies which we are largely unaware of in daily life.
2 It is important to let students lie quietly for a moment before getting up, and then tell them to get up slowly. Moving too quickly after an activity like this can undo much of the good it has done.
3 If the floor is unsuitable for lying on, or if space is limited, the activity can be done seated in chairs.

See also 4.2 Physical warm ups.

1.14 From seed to plant

Aim	To develop concentration, body awareness and muscular control
Level	All
Time	10 minutes
Preparation	Bring in some slow-tempo music (optional).

Procedure

1 Students find a space to stand in.
2 When you say *Go*, students curl up and make themselves as small and compact as they can. They are now a seed.
3 Then tell students to uncoil as slowly as possible into a plant reaching up towards the sun.

Notes

1 This is a good activity through which to introduce the idea of visualisation to the students. They should be told to close their eyes and visualise in their mind's eye how it is to be a seed, then progressively a plant. Visualisation is a powerful factor in language learning and is often overlooked in the rush to verbalisation.
2 It may be helpful to play some music to accompany the activity – something slow, which builds up towards a climax. Mahler, Sibelius or Brahms are all possibles but you may have some New Age music which you find more suitable.

1.15 Slow motion

Aim	To promote muscular control and awareness of shared space
Level	All
Time	10 minutes
Preparation	Bring in some slow-tempo music

Procedure

1 Clear the room so that students can move around easily. Students then form pairs.
2 As the music plays, each pair of students moves to it together, but in slow motion. They should try to coordinate their movements: sometimes this will mean making identical movements, sometimes one will make a movement which complements their partner's, e.g. one moves forward, the other back.
3 After a few minutes, students change partners and continue.

Notes

1 This is an excellent activity for developing students' ability to share the space harmoniously.

2 It is important that the pairs move not simply slowly, but in slow-motion, as if a film has been slowed right down. This obliges them to plan their movements much more consciously and carefully.

3 The main consideration when choosing the music is that the tempo should be slow.

See also 3.11 Normal, slow, fast.

1.16 Just relax

Aim	To help students to achieve a state of relaxation through concentration
Level	All
Time	10–15 minutes

Procedure

1 Students should either sit or lie down, with eyes closed.

2 Give any *one* of the following instructions:

- *Imagine you are under a luxurious, warm shower after a long, tiring day. Feel the water running all over you, washing away all the fatigue.*

- *Imagine you are sitting on the banks of a river deep in the countryside. It is summer. A wind is blowing gently. Think of all the sounds you can hear in this landscape.*

- *Sit comfortably. Now begin to rock from side to side very slowly and gently. Hum softly on a note.*

- *Imagine you can see an endless piece of black velvet in front of your eyes. Concentrate on it.*

- *Look at this diagram. Then close your eyes and try to see it in your mind's eye. Concentrate on it.*

 or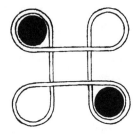

3 Bring the activity to a close by saying, gently but firmly: *Now it is time to come back. Start to get ready to open your eyes. Now open them, and stand up in your own time.*

Notes

1 The activity, when done properly, literally takes the student into another world of visualised sensations. It is powerfully relaxing, yet the student is in a state of high concentration too. Both conditions are valuable in unblocking mental capacity for learning.
2 Some groups may find this activity uncomfortable or just plain silly. If they really resist it, do something else and come back to try it on another occasion.
3 With groups which take well to the activity, use it on a regular basis as preparation for other learning activities.

See also 1.17 Directed relaxation, 1.27 Directed group visualisation, 7.6 Waking dream.

1.17 Directed relaxation

Aim	To bring the students to a state of alert relaxation in preparation for other activities
Level	All
Time	10 minutes

Procedure

1 Students stand comfortably, feet about shoulders' width apart, in their own space, with eyes closed.
2 Speaking in a calm, gentle, unhurried yet firm voice, say the following: *You are full of tension. It is like a fluid in your body. You are going to empty it away. Try to feel it in your head. Feel it flowing very slowly, downwards through your neck, your chest. Feel it flowing up your arms and then downwards ... down to the soles of the feet. Now you have small holes in each foot. Feel the tension draining away through the holes. Feel how relaxed you are now. Now you are going to draw in energy from the floor. As you breathe in, feel it flowing in through your feet, up your legs ... up to the crown of your head. Now feel how full of energy you are. When you are ready, open your eyes. How do you feel?*

Notes

1 Your voice quality is very important. It has to persuade the students to really feel the negative energy flowing out, and the positive energy flowing in. It is most important to speak slowly, allowing students time to focus on each part of their body as you refer to it.

2 This is an excellent way to re-energise a group who come to class tired or distracted (e.g. students who have come from another class, adults who have come in from work, etc.).

3 The activity can be done, with small adaptations, with students either lying down or sitting in chairs.

See also 1.27 Directed group visualisation, 7.6 Waking dream.

1.18 Going with the flow

Aim	To accustom students to the rhythms and cadences of English in a relaxing way
Level	All
Time	Up to 10 minutes
Preparation	Record a tape with one or more sequences of randomly repeated sentences. Each sequence is based on a different theme word. See Box 1 for two examples.

Procedure

1 Students sit, with eyes closed. Tell them that all they have to do is to listen; to let the words flow over them.

2 Play (or read) one of the sentence sequences (see Box 1).

Variation

1 Instead of the repeated sentences, choose some recordings of poetry in English. You need highly rhythmical pieces. Some possibilities include: Coleridge, *The Rime of the Ancient Mariner*; Keats, *Ode to Autumn*; Fitzgerald, *The Rubaiyat of Omar Khayyam*; Gerard Manley Hopkins, *Spring and Fall: to a young child*; Auden, *Night Mail*; Alfred Noyes, *The Highwayman*; anything of Dylan Thomas read by the author, etc. English literature is full of examples, many of which are now available on CDs. Again, it is important that students do not worry about the meaning – just the overall rhythmical effect.

2 After students have done the activity by simply listening, invite them to repeat the lines after you as you read them. You need to leave time for this between lines, of course.

Box 1

1 We have time.
   Time is something we have.
   Plenty of time.
   All the time in the world.
   Time without end.
   Plenty of time.
   Time is on our side.
   Time is standing still.
   We have time.
   All the time in the world.
   Plenty of time.
   Time unending.
   Time without end, etc.

2 It is quiet.
   So quiet.
   No noise.
   Not a sound.
   Everything is so still, so calm.
   Nothing is moving.
   There is no sound.
   The stillness is everywhere.
   Everything is so calm, so still, etc.

Notes

1 Again, the activity depends on voice quality. The recording (or the reading, if you decide to read it yourself) must be calmly rhythmical, almost mesmerising in its effect.
2 Emphasise that students should not try to understand everything they hear. It is enough just to let the words flow over them. It is the pulse, the underlying rhythm which they are absorbing sub-consciously.
3 The examples given are relatively simple but for more advanced learners, longer and more complex forms can be used.

See also 4.17 Group orchestration of texts.

Verbal exercises

1.19 Football wave

Aims	To build team spirit; to help students get to know each other's names
Level	All
Time	10–15 minutes
Preparation	Make sure you have enough large sheets of paper (A4 or larger) and felt-tip pens for all students

Procedure

1   Divide students into groups of about ten. Students write their name in capitals on a large piece of paper.
2   Students stand in a row holding their papers down. The student on the right starts by holding up his (or her) name above his head. All the team members call out his name as he does so. As he lowers his paper, the next student raises hers (or his) and everyone calls out her name. As she lowers hers … and so on. The effect should be like a wave rippling along the line of students (see illustration).

Notes

1   You will need to give students time to practise coordinating their wave.
2   This is a good 'getting to know you' activity for the start of a course.

Variation

Any number of different variations can be worked on this activity by changing what is written on the papers. It could be the occupations of the group members, their ages (where appropriate), what they like eating, their favourite pop star, etc.

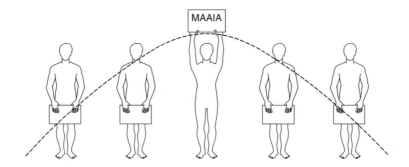

1.20 Can you do this?

Aims	To break the ice between members of a new group; to make everyone feel they can contribute something which interests the others
Focus	Expressions of interest/appreciation, e.g. *That's really interesting. How do you do that? Great!*
Level	All
Time	10 minutes plus

Procedure

1   Demonstrate something physical you can do (e.g. stand on one leg with your eyes shut). Then ask students to think of something physical they can do, which they demonstrate. Give them a couple of minutes to think about this. These 'tricks' may be something very simple, like raising just one eyebrow, making a popping sound by putting one finger in their mouth and pulling it out quickly; or something more complex, like a yoga position, wiggling ears, a simple magic trick, etc.

2   Students then work in pairs. One student demonstrates, the other tries to copy it. They take turns.

3   Students change partners and repeat the activity. Each student should work with about four different partners.

Note

You may like to ask for some of the more interesting 'tricks' to be demonstrated for the whole class at the end of the pairwork.

1.21 The sun and the moon

Aims	To break the ice with new groups; to encourage quick reactions to verbal stimuli
Focus	Simple paired vocabulary items
Level	Elementary and above
Time	10 minutes
Preparation	Come with a list of paired words or phrases, e.g. sun–moon, day–night, summer–winter, present–future, tortoise–hare, Saturday night–Sunday morning, etc.

Procedure

1   Students all stand together in the middle of the room.

2   Call out two words, indicating which end of the room corresponds with each, e.g. *Sun over there. Moon over there.* Students must choose

immediately which word they identify with, and go to the end of the room indicated.

3   When students are in two groups, one at the Moon end and the other at the Sun end, ask them to discuss with others in the same group, why they chose as they did. Then ask each Sun student to find one or more Moon students to discuss why they chose as they did.

Variation

Rather than having to choose between alternatives, ask students to position themselves according to likes/dislikes, e.g. one end of the room is 'very positive', the other is 'very negative'. Give the theme word, and students stand in the position, in the line, which corresponds to their feelings. (If the word was *green tea*, I would stand near the middle, as I do not have strong feelings either way.) The group then discuss why they stood where they did.

Note

Make sure that students make their choices immediately, on impulse. No dithering. This is what makes the choice interesting; it is only after the choice has been made that the student reflects on it in the discussion.

1.22 Back writing

Aim	To present words kinaesthetically, encouraging visualisation
Focus	Recycling of familiar vocabulary
Level	Elementary and above
Time	10 minutes

Procedure

1   Students work in pairs. One stands behind the other.
2   The student standing behind traces a simple word or short message on their partner's back with their forefinger. Their partner tries to interpret what has been written. Partners then change places.
3   After a couple of tries, change partners and repeat the activity.

Notes

1   Encourage students to interact verbally as the activity proceeds. Useful language will include: *Was that an 'A'? Can you please write it again? The first word/letter again, please. Can you go a bit more slowly, please?* etc.
2   Keep the activity simple to start with. Words or messages which are too long are difficult to interpret and will waste a lot of time.

3 You may want to use the activity to reinforce language already encountered in the coursebook. In this case, write the words or phrases on slips of paper and distribute them to the students.
4 Meeting words through an unusual sensory channel often helps to fix them in the memory.

Variation
Instead of words, students draw pictures.

1.23 Gobbledy-gook

Aims To get everyone warmed up vocally; to bond the group
Level All
Time 10 minutes

Procedure
1 Tell students that they are going to talk a completely unknown language for five minutes. They are to speak loudly and quickly, and with as much expression as possible. They should try to speak to at least three other students in turn. With each new partner, they have a brief conversation, taking turns as in a normal language.
2 Stop students after five minutes. They now repeat the activity, but this time they whisper their foreign language to others.

Variations
1 Students can be instructed to engage in specific interactions in their gobbledy-gook speak, e.g. asking and giving directions, asking the price of something, introducing oneself, etc.
2 You can ask one or two students to give a lecture on a given topic to the class using gobbledy-gook. Every so often, another student will 'interpret' the gobbledy-gook into English.

Notes
1 The main point of this activity is to get everyone interacting vigorously, and to warm up the vocal apparatus. Though it may seem a trifle bizarre, this activity does generate and release a great deal of energy.
2 Because this activity does not involve competence in a real language, everyone is on an equal footing.
3 The point of the whispering stage is to begin to calm down again after the excitement of the 'loud' stage.

See also 4.16 Listen to me!, Chapter 11, *Warming up*.

1.24 And I'm a butcher

Aims	To develop memory and careful listening; to have repetitive practice in a motivating framework; to foster group bonding
Focus	Vocabulary of occupations (and other lexical sets)
Level	All
Time	10–15 minutes

Procedure

1 Students sit in circles of 10–12, facing inwards.
2 One student starts by giving their name and an occupation, e.g. *I'm Ming, and I'm a butcher.* (The occupation does not have to be the real one. In fact, it is more entertaining if it is imaginary!) The next student on the right then says: *You're Ming, and you're a butcher. And I'm Carlos, and I'm a mechanic.* The next student then continues: *She's Ming, and she's a butcher. You're Carlos, and you're a mechanic. And I'm Slavka, and I'm a ballet dancer.* This continues round the circle until everyone has had a turn. The student who started then has to repeat the whole series.

Variation

You can vary the input to include other types of expressions and structures, e.g. *I'm X and I like …ing. I'm Y and I've just come back from Z. I'm N and I feel …,* etc.

Notes

1 Though the activity is repetitive, it generates a high degree of energy and attention.
2 It is better not to exceed 12 students per circle, otherwise the activity lasts too long and memory is overstretched.
3 Student self-esteem is raised by the activity. Each time a student's name is mentioned, it is as if they have been 'stroked'.

1.25 Let me tell you something about X

Aim	To facilitate mixing through the exchange of simple personal information
Focus	Eliciting information; reporting
Level	Elementary and above
Time	10–15 minutes

Procedure

1 Students walk around the room mixing freely.
2 When you give the word, students all have to find out one piece of personal information from as many others as possible in the space of five minutes.
3 Students sit in a circle and report on what they found out.

Notes

1 Stick to the five-minute deadline. This helps to ensure that students do not get stuck in a long conversation with any one person.
2 You can make the activity competitive; the winning student is the one who has information about the largest number of students (which he or she can recall accurately!).

See also 1.26 Something in common.

1.26 Something in common

Aim	To engage students in genuine interchange of personal information
Focus	Expression of likes/dislikes, memories, beliefs, opinions
Level	All
Time	15 minutes plus

Procedure

1 Ask students to note these four things:
   • a superstition you either do or don't believe in
   • a machine/mechanical device that really annoys you
   • anything which evokes a strong childhood memory
   • other people's habits which annoy you.
2 Students take two or three minutes to jot down what is true for them. They then circulate, comparing their own list with those of others. Students are especially looking for others who have similar responses to their own. Allow ten minutes for this. Students should try to make contact with as many others in the time as possible.
3 If there is time, students share their findings in a class feedback session.

Variation

You can vary the four things as much as you like, e.g. what scares me most, what relaxes me most, the thing I do best, the qualities I look for in a friend, etc. With elementary students, this can be very basic: my favourite food, colour, music, singer, sport, etc.

See also 1.25 Let me tell you something about X.

1. 27 Directed group visualisation

Aims	To develop visualisation of a story; to encourage careful listening
Focus	To be adjusted according to the specific story
Level	Intermediate and above
Time	15 minutes
Preparation	Rehearsal of the reading of a story (see Box 2 for an example), or preparation of an audio tape.

Procedure

1 Students lie down or sit comfortably, with their eyes closed. Let them know that you are going to tell them a story. Tell them they should try to visualise or feel the story in their minds' eye as you tell it.

2 Tell the story in a voice which expresses the appropriate feeling of the story as it develops.

3 Go on to a point where you feel the class can take over the story, then stop. Any student can then start to add to the development of the story.

Notes

1 Do not stop telling the story too soon. Students need time to get into the story line before you pass it to them.

2 When you stop, do not try to hurry students into contributing. It usually takes a couple of minutes before anyone speaks. Do not worry about this silence; it is productive silence.

3 Do not let the activity go on too long. If it starts to flag, tell students you will continue it another time. Alternatively, they can continue it as homework.

4 When the story is 'finished', you can ask students to dramatise it, preferably in groups.

5 The language level of the text can be adjusted to suit the level of the group. In the example in Box 2, only the present simple tense is used. Clearly, other tenses could have been used.

See also 1.16 Just relax, 7.6 Waking dream, Chapter 11, *Warming up*.

Box 2

You get down from the train. It moves away into the distance. You are alone. It is just a small country railway station, with the ticket clerk dozing under his newspaper, a fly buzzing on the window, roses and lilies growing sweet in the flower beds. You walk out of the station and into the afternoon sun. There is no village to be seen, not even a house; just a long, winding, dusty road disappearing into the forest. Time seems to have stopped. You walk slowly up the road and into the delicious cool of the shade under the trees. Now the road is straight, like a corridor through the dark forest. In the distance the road comes to an end with some very high iron gates. As you come nearer, you can see two large stone lions on each side of the gate. They remind you of the kind you have seen in photographs of the East. As you come to the gates, you notice there is a gatehouse to one side. It has high windowless stone walls, and a curving roof, like a Chinese temple. The only way in is through a dark archway. You hesitate for a moment, then walk into the pitch dark of the archway. Suddenly, your blood freezes. Something or someone is behind you ...

1.28 Childhood memories

Aims	To bond the group by the sharing of personal memories; to stimulate genuine oral interchanges
Focus	Past tense recounts
Level	All
Time	15–20 minutes

Procedure

1   Ask students to write down on a slip of paper a word which evokes a childhood memory. Suggest the following possible categories: a colour, a smell, a taste/flavour, a texture, a name (of a place, a person, an animal, a song, a book, etc.), a fruit, an object, a date or day, a year, etc. Tell students to avoid abstract words like *hope, courage,* etc.

2   Collect the slips of paper and redistribute them at random. Students circulate and try to find the person whose slip they now have. They can ask questions like: *Was yours about a date? Did you write about a smell?* etc. They should not show their slip to the other person. When they find who wrote the word on their slip, they sit down and ask for a full explanation, i.e. what is the precise memory represented by the word?

Variation

Students sit or lie down, with eyes closed. They are asked to think about a very vivid childhood memory in as much detail as possible – to recall the colours, smells, shapes, objects, people, etc. and their associations. Give enough time for this (at least five minutes). Students then form pairs and tell their partners about their childhood experience.

Notes

1 Memories shared are a powerful way of binding a group together. They become part of the group story. Care needs to be taken, however, not to urge students to share painful memories which they would rather keep to themselves.

2 It is usually best to use this activity only after the class has been together for a time, and a degree of trust established.

3 In a future lesson, you may wish to return to this activity, and to use some of the memory stories as the basis for dramatisation.

1.29 Personalities/celebrities

Aims	To ensure all members of the group mingle and interact; to set up genuine interaction
Focus	A range of question types
Level	Elementary and above
Time	15 minutes
Preparation	Write out enough small file cards for every student to have one. Write the names of famous people on the cards. Ideally cards should be in matched pairs, e.g. Batman–Robin, Mickey Mouse–Donald Duck, Caesar–Cleopatra, Darth Vadar–Obi-Wan Kenobi, Harry Potter–Lord Voldemort, Frodo–Gollum, etc.

Procedure

1 Distribute the cards at random to the students. They then circulate, trying to find out by indirect questioning who the other students are. They cannot ask *Who are you?* but need to use questions like: *Are you a living person? Are you American? Do you wear a mask?* etc. If possible, students try to find their 'partner', i.e. the person with the matching card.

2 After about ten minutes, have a feedback session where everyone is identified.

Variation
You can prepare the cards as above. In class, pin or stick cards to the
students' backs. They then circulate, trying to find out who they are by
asking questions of the students who can see their card.

Note
You may need to demonstrate with one student the kinds of questions they
should use, before letting students loose with the cards.

Group formation activities

1.30 Strings

Aim	To form pairs or groups randomly
Level	All
Time	3 minutes
Preparation	Bring in 50-cm-lengths of string – half as many as there are students in the class.

Procedure

1 Hold the strings in your hand (see illustration). Invite students all to take
   hold of one end of one piece of string. When you let go of the strings,
   students holding the same piece of string are paired off.

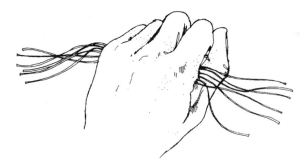

2 If you need groups of four, repeat the process. This time each pair takes
   one string.

Note
It is sometimes desirable to group students randomly, otherwise they only
tend to work with other students they like or know. By randomising the
group-formation process, you can get a better mix.

1.31 Atom 3!

Aim	To form groups of whatever size is required; to ensure lively mixing
Level	All
Time	5–10 minutes
Preparation	Bring in a CD/tape of some lively music.

Procedure

1   Students move freely around the room to the music.

2   When you stop the tape, call out *Atom 3!* Students then have to form groups of three with others nearest to them.

3   Restart the music and continue. Next time you stop the tape, call out *Atom …* (whatever number you like). Students again form groups of this number.

4   Finally, call out the number you want the groups to be in for the next activity.

1.32 Mix and mingle

Aim	To form more or less random groups
Level	All
Time	5 minutes
Preparation	Bring in a CD/tape of some music (optional).

Procedure

1   Play some music, if you have any. Students then simply walk around the space freely.

2   When you give the word, or when the music stops, each student takes the hand of the person nearest to them.

3   The pairs then stay together as you restart the activity. When the music stops, each pair takes the hands of the nearest pair to them. They are then in groups of four. Continue if you want groups of eight.

1.33 I've got my eye on you!

Aim	To pair students using non-verbal expression
Level	All
Time	5–10 minutes

Procedure

1 Students stand in two lines facing each other about two metres apart (an equal number of students in each line).
2 Tell students to look carefully at all the students in the other line, without looking at any one person for too long.
3 Then ask students to decide on one person in the opposite line they would like to partner. They then try to attract the attention of that person purely through eye contact and facial expression.
4 When you give the word, the pairs go to stand together.
5 If you need groups of four, repeat the activity. This time, the pairs have to attract the attention of another pair in the opposite line.

Note
It is possible that more than one student on one side may be interested in the same student on the other side. If this happens, it will be the one who makes contact first who gets the partner. The unlucky student will then have to find someone else.

1.34 I know what I like

Aim	To form compatible groups through exchange of genuine information
Level	All
Time	15 minutes

Procedure

1 Each student writes on a slip of paper three things they like very much, and three things they really dislike.
2 Students then circulate freely, trying to find someone who shares as many likes and dislikes as possible. (They do not need to share all the same likes and dislikes; just one or two will do.) These pairs then go on looking for others with similar likes and dislikes until groups are formed.

Variation
You can adapt the level of difficulty to the level of the students, e.g. with elementary-level students, you could restrict the likes and dislikes to food items, or colours, or sports, etc.; with slightly higher levels, you could limit it to things they like doing, or places they like going, etc.

Note
Make sure the students ask each other questions. They should not simply show their slips of paper to each other.

2 Observation

When actors communicate on stage, they need to be acutely aware of each other. This awareness is based on careful observation of what is going on, including noticing where others are standing and how, their facial expressions, their tone of voice, and how the space is arranged. Observation is the key to anticipation. And anticipating what is going to happen, and what is going to be said, is critical for good dramatic communication. Language learners are not actors, but for them to communicate effectively they also need to develop awareness through observation. It is alarming to reflect that so much of what goes on around us is unnoticed, taken for granted, stereotyped in our minds. The activities in this section aim to promote observation in the service of better communication. They also provide genuine opportunities to interact meaningfully in the foreign language.

2.1 Freeze!

Aim	To develop awareness of physical position relative to other people in the group
Focus	The language of location: *near, far, to the left/right, over there, next to, on the opposite side*, etc.
Level	All
Time	15 minutes
Preparation	Clear space so that students can move around freely. You will need a cassette recorder and some taped music.

Procedure

1 Students move around freely as the music plays. When it stops, they must freeze in the position they are in at the time.
2 Students hold their positions till the music starts again. They then move around again.
3 When you stop the music next, students must all return to their previous position in the room, and freeze in the posture they were in earlier.
4 Students form groups of about four with students near them. They then discuss how and where they were standing, how easy or difficult it was to recall, and how accurately they and others managed to refreeze.

Notes

1 With some groups, you may find it better to inform them of what they will have to do before starting the activity. With others, you may simply spring the activity on them as a surprise.
2 Encourage students to observe each other critically, as well as themselves.
3 If you feel it will be helpful, round up with a brief class discussion.
4 Try repeating the activity at the end of the class to see how easy or difficult students find it to take up their original positions again after a time interval.

See also 2.3 Say 'Cheese'.

2.2 Back-to-back

Aim	To develop close observation of another person
Focus	Language of personal description: physical features, clothing, etc.
Level	All
Time	15 minutes

Procedure

1 Students work in pairs. They are told to observe their partner very carefully for two minutes.
2 Students then stand back-to-back, so that they can no longer see their partners. They take it in turns to describe their partner in as much detail as possible from memory.
3 As they are being described, students may give feedback, or ask for more detailed descriptions, e.g. A: *You're wearing glasses.* B: *Are the frames metal or plastic?*
4 When both partners have finished, they turn to face each other again and evaluate the accuracy of their descriptions.

Variation

Students are asked to carefully observe the room they are in and to remember it in as much detail as possible. In pairs, one student, with eyes closed, answers questions from the other about the room. *How many windows are there?* etc. Students then change places. The former questioner keeps eyes closed. This time, the partner asks questions about their own appearance, e.g. *Am I wearing a watch?* This shock tactic usually shows how little we observe about people near to us.

Notes

1 You may wish to do some revision of vocabulary before starting this activity, to ensure that students have the necessary descriptive terms.

2 If there is time, ask students to change partners and repeat the activity. Were they more accurate the second time around?

2.3 Say 'Cheese'

Aim	To develop careful observation of space/relative position
Focus	Language of position: *right/left*, *nearer the front/back*, *next to*, *behind*, etc.
Level	All
Time	20 minutes

Procedure

1 Students work in groups of about eight. Two groups will work together.

2 Group 1 arranges itself for a group photograph (students can be as outrageous as they like in the facial expressions they put on, clothing changes, etc.). Group 2 carefully observes this group photograph.

3 Group 2 also poses for a photograph, observed carefully by Group 1.

4 Group 2 then has to reconstitute Group 1, in exactly the way they were posing for their group photograph, by giving them oral instructions.

5 Finally, Group 1 reconstitutes Group 2 in the same way.

Notes

1 You may need to revise some of the positional vocabulary before getting started.

2 Make sure students reconstitute the groups by oral instructions only; no physical pushing around!

See also 2.1 Freeze!

2.4 Just listening

Aim	To sharpen awareness of the many sounds which surround us
Focus	Vocabulary for describing sounds, e.g. *sharp*, *dull*, *high*, *low*, *shrill*, *buzzing*, *humming*, *knocking*, *it sounded*, etc.
Level	All
Time	10 minutes

Procedure

1 Ask students to close their eyes. For two minutes, they simply listen to all the sounds going on around them.
2 Students then open their eyes and note down all the sounds they heard.
3 Students report on what they heard to the whole class. Encourage them to expand on each sound, e.g.
   A: *I heard the sound of traffic.*
   B: *Anything in particular?*
   A: *I heard a motorbike.*
   B: *What was it doing?*
   A: *Making a very loud vrooming noise.*
   etc.

Follow-on

1 Students work in pairs. As homework, they prepare a 'sound-script'. That is, they decide on a sequence of sounds they will make in the classroom. In class, each pair presents its sound-script while the others listen, with eyes closed. If possible, students should make their own sound recording and play that. This is followed by interpretations and comments from the whole group about what they heard.
2 This activity can lead very naturally into an extended discussion of the role of noise in our industrialised, consumerist society, e.g. the music played in supermarkets, the damaging effects of noise pollution, the effects of mobile phones, etc.

Note

You may wish deliberately to add a few sounds of your own, e.g. tapping a glass, dropping your pen, sniffing, clearing your throat, etc.

2.5 I said, he said, she said ...

Aim	To sharpen observation and accurate recall of what someone else actually said
Focus	Past tense narrative; literal reported speech: *You/She said: '....'*
Level	All
Time	30 minutes

Procedure

1 Students work in groups of three. In each group, Student A tells a story about an incident in their life (a childhood memory, a recent event, etc.).

This should not last more than five minutes. Student B listens carefully and makes notes if necessary. Student C does the same.

2 Student B then retells the story as accurately as possible. Students A and C listen carefully to the retelling.

3 Student C then comments on Student B's retelling. How accurate, how complete was it? Student A can be asked questions to verify what was said but should not interrupt.

4 Each student has a chance to play A, B and C.

Notes

1 You can set the preparation for this activity as a homework task. This saves time in class.

2 Consider using some of the more interesting stories as the basis for role-play activities later in the course.

Follow-on

If there is time, have a feedback session where the more interesting stories are shared.

See also 1.28 Childhood memories.

2.6 Minimal differences

Aim	To develop sensitivity to small changes in a message: syntactical or lexical
Focus	Changes of tense form; words with similar but different phonological forms, e.g. *Thailand/Taiwan*
Level	All
Time	20 minutes plus
Preparation	You will need to prepare enough (different) sentences written out on slips of paper for each student to have one, e.g. *I chose to go to Taiwan.*

Procedure

1 In groups of six to eight, students are each given one sentence on a slip of paper (they all have different sentences). They do not show it to anyone else.

2 Each student then reads their sentence aloud to the group. They repeat their sentences twice.

3 Each student then has to think of a way to slightly change their sentence. As they read it, others in the group try to notice how it has been changed.

Follow-on

If there is time, write up some of the changes on the board as revision of tense forms, vocabulary, etc.

Variation

Give students sentences which allow for the shifting of stress from one word to another, e.g. *I put his car away in the garage last night.* Students then decide on two or three different sentence stresses. The others must decide where the stress was put, and what difference it made to the meaning, e.g. *I put HIS car away in the garage last night* (not yours), *I put his CAR away in the garage last night* (not his motorbike), etc.

Notes

1 The example sentence in Preparation could be modified in many ways: *I choose to go ..., I've chosen to go ..., I chose to fly ..., I chose to go to Thailand*, etc.

2 You may find it helpful to give out the sentences as homework, so that students have time to prepare the changes they plan to make.

See also 4.12 Shifting the stress.

2.7 My potato

Aim	To develop close observation of small differences
Focus	Expressions to convey shape, size, texture, colour, etc. and to show small differences, e.g. *slightly, just a bit, not much ..., not very ...,* etc.
Level	All
Time	20 minutes plus
Preparation	You will need to bring enough potatoes (or other items – see Variation) to class for each student to have one.

Procedure

1 Students work in groups of six to eight. Place the potatoes in a pile for each group. Each student in the group takes one. They spend at least five minutes examining their potato very closely. They then replace it in the pile. The pile is then covered with a cloth or piece of paper.

2 Students write down details which will help them to remember their potato.

3 Students uncover the potatoes and try to find their own potato again.

4 Each student explains to the others in the group how they identified the potato again.

Variation

Potatoes are ideal but you can decide to use corks, bottle tops, sea shells (all the same kind), pebbles/stones, leaves, flowers (of the same kind), or any other object which can only be distinguished through minimal differences. At the end of the activity, ask students to write a 'praise song' for their potato (or other object) in which they extol its beauty and other qualities, e.g.:

Your skin is smoother than cream.
Your shape is so regular –
That you fit perfectly in the palm of my hand.
But most of all I love your two black eyes.

Students then recite their praise songs for their group.

Notes

1   It is important to give students enough time to really 'get inside' their objects. As Blake wrote: *To see a world in a grain of sand, And a heaven in a wild flower.*

2   You may like to remind students that we often overlook small items which are of key importance. This is particularly true of communication, where a slight inflection or change of facial expression can completely change the meaning.

See also 2.8 Kim's game, 4.17 Group orchestration of texts.

2.8 Kim's game

Aim	To develop accurate visual memory
Focus	Vocabulary of location; also of size, shape, colour, etc.
Level	All
Time	20 minutes plus
Preparation	Make sure that you have a large flat surface, such as a tabletop, and a cloth to cover it. Bring to class an assortment of about 25 objects, such as a light bulb, a screwdriver, a corkscrew, a foreign coin, a postcard, a box of matches, etc.

Procedure

1   Place the objects at random on the flat surface. Invite students to gather round and look carefully at the objects.

2   After about five minutes, cover the objects with a cloth.

3   Students work individually to make a list of all the objects they can recall.

4   Students work in pairs to check their lists. They then help you, the teacher, to make a complete list on the board.

5   Finally, unveil the objects, and let students check how accurately they recalled the objects.

6   In feedback, ask students how they recalled the objects. Was it by position? By colour? By association (all sharp objects together, etc.)?

Variations

1   Instead of bringing objects to class, you can ask each student to contribute one object from their personal belongings. When students have recalled the objects covered, they can also try to guess which object belongs to which student.

2   Repeat the activity up to step 4 above. However, while students are engaged in step 3, unobtrusively remove some objects, or change their location, or add one or two new ones. Then continue as before. When students have noticed the changes, cover the objects again. This time, students not only have to recall the objects, but give a precise description of each one.

Note

Though the objects may not be of much intrinsic interest, the moment they are removed from view, the activity becomes challenging. If the activity is going well, encourage a longer discussion.

See also 2.7 My potato.

2.9 Familiar scenes

Aim	To develop sharper awareness of the local environment
Focus	Descriptive terms (size, colour, shape, etc.) and the vocabulary of location
Level	All
Time	20 minutes class time, plus homework time

Procedure

1   Students will work in pairs. As homework, each pair must prepare a list of questions based on features of the town they are in. These might include:
   • the exact colour of post-boxes, and any words or symbols on them
   • the shape, colour and design of well-known stores
   • the number, colour and arrangement of seats on local buses or trains
   • details of any local statues or monuments
   • what the road or pavement surfaces are like

- the precise location and appearance of traffic signs
- the names of all the shops near the school
- the precise wording of prominent signs or notices near the school.

Students should also make sure they know the answers to their questions!

2   In class, each pair works with another pair, asking and answering the
    questions.

Variation

If students are long-time inhabitants of their town, you may ask them to do
the activity 'cold' – that is, without preparing it as homework. If they get any
answers wrong, they must find the correct information as homework.

Notes

1   You will need to familiarise yourself with your locality too!
2   With classes who may be newcomers to your country or town, this
    activity is an excellent way for them to familiarise themselves with their
    new locality.

2.10 Like me? Like you?

Aim	To develop close observation of a partner, and notice similarities and differences
Focus	Language of personal description, and of similarity/difference, e.g. *You've got … whereas I …, Our … are the same colour, My … is shorter than …*, etc.
Level	Beginner–Intermediate
Time	15 minutes

Procedure

1   Students work in pairs. They begin by noting on a piece of paper three
    ways they think they are different from their partner, and three ways they
    are similar or the same. Set a time limit for this.
2   Partners then exchange their papers and decide how accurate their
    opinions are.
3   Finally, they report back to the whole class.

Follow-on

The activity can be extended by asking students to decide on one feature in
their partner which they wish they had, e.g. *I wish I had green eyes like
yours.*

Variation

If class members do not yet know each other very well, give them five minutes, in pairs, to find out at least three things they share with their partner. These do not have to be things to do with physical appearance.

Note

With lower level learners, it will be best to concentrate on physical features, clothing, etc. More advanced groups can be asked to focus on personality, interests, opinions, etc.

See also 1.25 Let me tell you something about X, 1.26 Something in common.

2.11 First this, then that …

Aim	To develop close observation of a series of actions
Focus	Sequencing language: *first, next, after that, before that, at the same time as* …, etc.; past simple tense narrative
Level	All
Time	20 minutes plus
Preparation	Before the class, decide on a sequence of about 15 actions which you will perform in a particular order. It is best to note these down to make sure recall is accurate.

Procedure

1 In class, tell students that they should carefully observe what you do in the coming five minutes. They may take notes if they wish.

2 Carry out your sequence of actions, e.g. walk to the door, bend down to pick something up, look pointedly at a given spot on the wall, rummage in your pocket for something, etc.

3 As soon as you finish, ask the class to form groups of three. Each group must agree on the sequence of actions you performed. Allow five minutes for this.

4 Collect feedback from all groups. They should report not only on what you did but on the way you did it, e.g. *You bent down very slowly*.

5 Students nominate one student per group to repeat the sequence of actions as accurately as possible. The whole class gives feedback, including 'corrections' to students after they have completed their version of the sequence.

6 Finally, repeat your sequence for everyone to check.

Follow-on

1 In a later class, you may like to ask students to prepare their own
   sequences to perform.
2 You can conduct a discussion based on the reliability of our memory for
   what we have seen. What effects does this have in a court of law, for
   example? How can we be so sure that what we 'remember' is what we
   actually observed?

Note

You may be surprised at the amount of disagreement there is about
something so simple as a sequence of ordinary actions. This provides rich
input for the discussion.

See also 2.1 Freeze!, 2.3 Say 'Cheese'.

2.12 Picture memory

Aim	To develop accurate memory for detail
Focus	Language of location: *in the bottom right-hand corner*, etc.; descriptive language of colour, size, shape, etc.
Level	All
Time	Up to 30 minutes
Preparation	You will need to prepare enough pictures for each group of four to have one. The pictures should contain a lot of detail and action. The pictures painted by Hieronymous Bosch and by Pieter Breughel are good examples. Auguste Renoir's *Le Moulin de la Galette* is another good one. Beryl Cook's pictures are also a more modern possibility. But the important thing is to ensure that there is plenty going on in the pictures.

Procedure

1 Distribute the pictures, one per group of four. Students spend five to ten
   minutes looking at the picture together, discussing all the details they
   notice.
2 Collect the pictures from each group. They must now try to reconstitute
   the picture by describing it in as much detail as possible. One group
   member acts as note-taker. If any students are gifted artists, they may try
   to redraw parts of the picture.
3 Conduct a whole-class feedback session. How much detail was recalled?
4 Finally, redistribute the pictures so that groups can check the accuracy of
   their recall.

Notes

1   The first time you try this activity, it is better that all groups have the same picture. Later, you may try giving each group a different picture.

2   With less advanced groups, it may be useful to review useful language such as: *at the top/bottom, in the middle, in the corner,* etc. With more advanced groups, you may wish to teach some basic art vocabulary, e.g. *in the foreground/background, perspective,* etc., and more detailed colour vocabulary such as *ochre, vermilion,* etc.

See also 6.14 Recreating the scene.

3 Working with mime

Mime activities can provide a real stimulus to the imagination. From visual clues alone we have to construct a message. This is a powerful process both for those carrying out the mime, who have to project themselves through movement and gesture only, and for those who try to interpret it. For both, a degree of visualisation is involved. The importance of visualisation in language learning has been emphasized in recent years.

Mime has other advantages, too. It uses different sensory inputs – visual and kinaesthetic – in support of the purely verbal. It seems to spark off a process of mental rehearsal of the language required (see 3.14 Hotel receptionist for a good example of this). Mime also highlights and underlines the importance of the non-verbal aspects of communication. It draws attention to the complex partnership between verbal and non-verbal by, temporarily, withdrawing the verbal. Mime also calls for close observation of small particulars (see Chapter 2).

And, like most of the activities in this book, mime generally involves no expensive or elaborate equipment – just a roomful of human beings.

3.1 What am I doing?

Aim	To introduce the idea of mime as a form of expression
Focus	Present continuous to describe ongoing actions, e.g. *You're fishing*; expressions for eliciting more detailed responses, e.g. *Yes, but where am I fishing? What am I trying to catch?*
Level	All
Time	15 minutes plus
Preparation	Make enough cards so that there is one for each student. Boxes 3 and 4 provide some examples of cards for an elementary group and an advanced group.

Procedure
1　Students work in pairs. Each student is given one of the cards, which they must not show to their partner.
2　Students take it in turns to mime the item on their card. It is the partners' job to interpret the mime as accurately as possible, and to ask questions to clarify anything which is not clear.

Box 3　Elementary

You are in the middle of a frozen lake, fishing through a hole in the ice.

You are trying to stay awake in a boring lesson.

You are in a crowded train, trying to read someone else's newspaper.

You are in bed in the dark in a strange house. You are trying to find the light switch near your bed.

You are watching a football match on TV. Your team is losing.

You are trying to eat with chopsticks. It is the first time you have used them.

You are waiting for the last bus. There are lots of people and you know they will not all be able to get on. Some of them are trying to jump the queue.

You are in a big store. When you get to the pay counter, you discover that you have lost your money.

Box 4   Advanced

You are trying to fill in an immigration form on an aeroplane. There is a lot of turbulence, the meal tray is still in front of you, and you have a very fat man on each side of you.

You are trying several ways to get your car keys, which you have dropped into a drain in the street.

You are a tightrope walker halfway across Niagara Falls. You suddenly feel a sneeze coming on.

You are dancing the tango with your boss's wife (husband) who is very large and who does not know the steps.

You are in a very crowded underground train during the rush hour. You feel someone's hand in your pocket but you cannot decide whose it is.

You are an Italian film director, trying to show the two lead actors how to kiss in the way you want them to.

You have been trying on a very tight pair of jeans. You have managed to squeeze into them – but you cannot get out of them again!

You are at a very important business lunch. Your host has just ordered a local speciality (fried locusts). You feel sick but it will offend your host if you do not eat them!

Notes
1   This is an activity which might be used to get students started on mime. Later, they can be asked to devise their own situations.
2   You may need to help out by providing some of the language for questioning.

See also 3.4 Difficulty with large or small objects.

3.2 My word

Aim	To reinforce vocabulary items through mime
Focus	Selected vocabulary you wish to reactivate
Level	All
Time	15–20 minutes (repeated at intervals)
Preparation	You need to prepare word cards bearing the items of vocabulary you want students to revise. These may be highly concrete, e.g. *apple*, *knife*, *key*, etc. or, at higher levels, more conceptually challenging, e.g. *futile*, *sly*, *deliberately*, *slither*, etc. You need enough different cards for at least one per student.

Procedure
1   Begin by demonstrating one or two mimes yourself. Students guess what you have mimed. Whoever guesses correctly is given a card and takes the next turn to mime.
2   Distribute one card each to every student. Students will work in pairs.
3   Partners take it in turns to try to convey their word through mime. Encourage students to interact orally at this stage by asking for repetition, making suggestions, asking questions, etc.
4   When partners have guessed each other's word, they join another pair and repeat the activity. By this time, students should have become more adept at miming their words.
5   Students then exchange cards with the other pair, and continue the activity with a different pair of students.

Variation
With younger learners or beginners using concrete items, you may prefer to use pictures rather than words – but when the words are guessed, it has to be in English.

Note

The activity is equally useful with beginners and advanced students. In fact, it can be a lot more interesting with more advanced groups, since they are better able to talk about what they do.

3.3 Metronome mime

Aim	To describe a sequence of mimed actions
Focus	Past simple tense narrative to describe actions; language of speculation, e.g. *It looks as if ..., I wonder if ..., Maybe ...,* etc.
Level	All
Time	20–30 minutes
Preparation	Bring in a metronome if you have one.

Procedure

1 Students work in pairs. They mime a series of actions you dictate to them, e.g. cutting bread, drinking a cup of hot coffee, eating a bowl of cereal.
2 Repeat the same series of actions, but this time, students must move in time to the slow and regular beat of a metronome. (You do not actually need a metronome. Instead, you can clap your hands to the speed of the beat you want, or make a clicking sound with your tongue, or knock two stones together.) Each pair should try to synchronise movements.
3 Each pair of students decides on some actions of their own. They rehearse these, face to face, trying to synchronise their metronome movements, as if one of them is the mirror image of the other.
4 Each pair joins another pair and presents their metronome mime for interpretation and evaluation.

Note

It is important that students make the movements as precise as possible. For the mime to be really effective, students need to 'feel' the weight, texture, shape and size of the objects being mimed. All too often, the tendency is to go for a sort of shorthand, idealised, stereotypical gesture rather than the fully realised one.

See also 1.15 Slow motion, 3.11 Normal, slow, fast.

3.4 Difficulty with large or small objects

Aim	To sharpen awareness of objects which surround us, and their obstinate resistance to our control over them!
Focus	Present progressive tense to describe ongoing actions (including the question form *Are you ...ing ...?*); asking for additional information, e.g. *Does it have a ...? Are there any ... on it?* etc.
Level	Elementary–Intermediate (though even Advanced students get a lot from it)
Time	15–20 minutes

Procedure

1   Students work in groups of four. Each group decides on, or is given, a number of situations involving small objects and the kinds of difficulty they might have with them. Here are some examples:
   - tying a shoelace with thick gloves on
   - getting a goldfish out of a bowl with fingers
   - trying to get a small key off a very stiff key ring
   - opening a bottle without a bottle opener
   - getting a splinter out of your backside
   - putting a miniaturised battery in an alarm clock.

2   Students practise their mimes of these situations. When they are ready, they join another group of four, and each group presents their mime. The other group tries to interpret the mime and asks for supplementary information to clarify anything which is not clear.

Variations

1   Instead of a small object, students choose a very large object. Here are some examples:
   - carrying a grand piano down some narrow stairs
   - removing a fallen tree across a road
   - lifting a car to clear the way in a street
   - lowering a very heavy box into a deep hole
   - erecting a large tent in a storm
   - trying to manoeuvre a very long ladder against a building
   - erecting a bronze statue.

The sequence is then repeated as in step 2.

2 Students choose to mime the moving of a very precious, fragile object. Here are some examples:
- some ancient scrolls found in a cave, which could crumble at the slightest touch
- a very large Ming dynasty vase
- the last butterfly of a species
- a mummified body
- a dinosaur's egg
- a mousetrap with a very sensitive spring
- a rifle with a hair trigger
- a premature baby.

Notes
1 Students should again be reminded that the more precisely observed their mime is, the better.
2 Encourage students to both evaluate the mimes they see, and to ask probing questions about them.

See also 3.1 What am I doing?

3.5 Exchanging objects

Aim	To increase awareness of the physical qualities of objects, and stimulate discussion of them
Focus	Vocabulary of size, weight, shape and texture; clarification questions
Level	Elementary–Intermediate
Time	20 minutes

Procedure
1 Students work in pairs, facing each other.
2 Each student takes two or three minutes to think of an object small enough for them to hold.
3 Students take it in turns to mime how they would handle their object for their partners, e.g. holding a small kitten. This is done in complete silence.
4 Students hand over their imaginary object to their partners, who receive it as realistically as possible.
5 Pairs discuss what they think they have received, and make comments on the accuracy of each other's mimes.

Notes

1 Encourage students to be imaginative in their choice of objects, not simply to make easy, clichéd choices. Here are some examples:

- a hair drier
- an energy-saving light bulb
- a rubber band
- a packet of crisps
- a pepper mill
- a toilet roll
- a pocket calculator
- a corkscrew
- a postage stamp
- a credit card
- a piece of sandpaper
- a packet of tissues.

2 Students should also be encouraged to mime their objects as precisely as possible.

3.6 Taste, touch, smell …

Aim To use mime to reinforce the language of the senses
Focus Language associated with the senses, e.g. *It tastes (of)*, *It feels (like)*, *It smells (like)*, etc.; evaluative expressions, e.g. *I liked the way …*, *I'm not sure why you …*, *I think it would have been better if you'd …*, etc.
Level Elementary–Intermediate
Time 15–20 minutes plus

Procedure

1 Students work in groups of five. Each group decides on something to eat. Together, they work out a way of miming eating their chosen item of food, and practise doing it once or twice. Here are some examples:

- spaghetti
- a very hot curry
- chilli peppers
- a very tough steak
- raw eggs.
- pizza
- shellfish
- a fish with a lot of bones
- fried grasshoppers

2 One member from each group then goes to the next group. The newcomer to each group carries out the mime, and the group tries to identify what it is, and evaluates the performance. One member of the group then carries out that group's mime and the newcomer tries to identify it, and evaluates the performance.

Variations
1 Repeat the above sequence with the sense of touch. Here are some
   examples:
   - sticky tape
   - bread dough
   - a silk shirt
   - wet trousers
   - a hot dish
   - a hard chair
   - animal fur
   - wet paint
   - rough tree bark
   - a slimy frog
   - an unshaven chin
   - a sharp thorn.
2 Repeat the sequence with the sense of smell. Here are some examples:
   - unwashed socks
   - cigar smoke
   - bad eggs
   - ripe apples
   - mothballs
   - French perfume.
   - stale breath
   - rotten fish
   - fresh bread
   - horse manure
   - old books
3 Repeat the sequence, but this time students focus on miming listening to
   something. Here are some examples:
   - a boring lecture
   - a lover's conversation
   - someone talking on a mobile phone
   - eavesdropping on a conversation on an aeroplane
   - a political speech
   - a sermon in church
   - a Shakespeare play
   - a pop concert
   - a phone call bringing you good/bad news
   - an accusation from a lawyer in court
   - an unfunny comedian on stage.

Note
Remind students that they should try to think themselves into the total
context of their mimes: Who are they? Where are they? Why are they doing
what they are doing? What time of day is it? Encourage them to ask each
other questions relating to these contextual features.

3.7 What time of day is it?

Aim	To show, through mime, activities typical of certain time periods in the day
Focus	Time vocabulary, including both actual times (e.g. *10.30am*), and periods (e.g. *in the early hours of the morning, coffee break*, etc.); present continuous for actions going on before our eyes, e.g. *You're directing the traffic*
Level	Elementary–Intermediate
Time	15–20 minutes
Preparation	Write the names of professions (e.g. fashion model, football star, pop idol, butcher, policeman, etc.) on cards – enough cards for one card per group.

Procedure

1 Students work in groups of three. Each group takes one of the profession cards.

2 Groups discuss their character, and decide on a time of day for that person. They must then agree an action appropriate to their character at that time of day, e.g. *shopkeeper/8pm – pulling down the steel shutters and locking up.*

3 Groups practise their mime. They then join another group, and one person from each group performs their mime. The other group has to guess the person, the activity, and the time based on the mime they see. Groups then comment on each other's mimes.

Variations

1 More advanced groups can be asked to add two more elements to their mime: a geographical locality, and a mood, e.g. the mime might then be of a traffic policeman in Bangkok during the rush hour, in a very bad mood.

2 See Variation 1. Instead of performing their own mime, groups simply write down the description of the character, the time of day, the place, the action and the mood on a slip of paper. Groups then exchange their slips and work out a mime based on the descriptions they have been given.

Notes

1 Encourage students to engage in discussion and questioning of each other's mimes.

2 If the class is not too large, every group may be asked to perform its mime for the whole class.

3.8 Mimes from the past

Aim	To use past incidents as a stimulus for mime/interpretation activities
Focus	Past tense narration; speculative expressions/modals
Level	Intermediate and above
Time	30 minutes plus

Procedure

1 Give students ten minutes to recall an event that sticks in their mind from their own past, which could be mimed, e.g. arriving late for school or for an important meeting; falling over while dancing with the most beautiful girl at the dance; falling asleep in class and being caught; shoplifting something useless and being caught by the store detective; being given a new bicycle for their birthday, etc.

2 Students then work in groups of three. They take turns to perform their mime of the event. Their partners try to interpret the mime and to get more details about the incident through questioning.

Follow-on

If there is time, students guess the adjective which best describes the person's feelings about the mimed incident, e.g. *delighted*, *guilty*, *embarrassed*, *scared*, etc. You can either list possible adjectives for them to choose from, or let them find their own.

Variation

In groups of four or five, students decide on a famous historical incident or myth from their own culture or from world culture. They then work out a mime of the incident, which they perform for another group. The other group tries to interpret the mime, and asks supplementary questions, e.g. (for Greek students) *Why did Socrates agree to drink the poison? How often did Archimedes take a bath?* etc.

Note

If students have difficulty coming up with incidents, you may have to prompt them: *A present you received? Something that disappointed you? A surprise visit from someone? A punishment you received?* etc.

See also 1.28 Childhood memories.

3.9 Miming a poem

Aim	To enhance understanding of a text through miming its content
Focus	This will depend on the content of the text, and can be tailored to suit a particular class's need at a particular time
Level	Pre-Intermediate and above
Time	One class hour
Preparation	Copy the texts of enough poems so that each pair or group has a different one. Boxes 5 and 6 provide two possibilities: one simple, one more complex.

Procedure

1 Divide the class into pairs or groups. The group size will depend on the way you decide to divide up the text. In *One, Two* ... there might be five: one student per line. In *Commuter* there could be five: one student per verse.

2 Give each group a copy of the text. Groups have 15 minutes to prepare a mime version of the text.

3 Each group joins another group. They do not show their texts to each other. They take turns to perform their mime for the other group, who try to work out what the 'story' is by asking questions, making suggestions, etc.

4 Each group gives its text to the other group. Groups comment on how accurately each other's mime reflected the content of the text. Groups then perform their mimes again, making changes if they wish. The other group again has to decide how accurate a representation of the text has been given.

Follow-on

In a later class, or as a homework assignment, groups work on producing a version of the story with words – a playscript – which can then be performed.

Notes

1 It would be helpful to gradually build up a collection of shortish texts for use with this activity.

2 The activity helps students 'apprehend' the poem as well as merely to 'comprehend' the poem; that is to say, they 'get inside' the poem rather than understanding it from the outside only. By having to decide on how to mime the poem, students are engaging more than one sensory channel, which reinforces their understanding of the text.

3 You may, of course, choose short prose extracts as well as poems. These should have a clear action line from beginning to end. Spy thrillers and detective stories are a good source.

See also 4.17 Group orchestration of texts.

Box 5

One, two, tie up my shoe.
Three, four, knock at the door.
Five, six, pick up sticks.
Seven, eight, lay them straight.
Nine, ten, start all over again.

Box 6   Commuter

He lives in a house in the suburbs.
He rises each morning at six.
He runs for the bus to the station,
Buys his paper and looks at the pics.

He always gets in the same carriage,
Puts his briefcase up on the rack,
Thinks miserably of his office,
And knows he can never turn back.

He gets to his desk by nine thirty,
Wondering what he should do.
When the coffee break comes at eleven,
He knows he still hasn't a clue.

His lunch break is quite uninspiring,
He sits it out in the canteen.
It's fish and chips, mince or potatoes,
A choice that's quite literally obscene.

At five he runs back to the station,
Gets in the same carriage again,
Unfolds his evening paper,
Pulls a veil down over his brain.

ALAN MALEY

3.10 Miming noises

Aim	To represent sounds uniquely through mime, thus engaging more than one sensory channel
Focus	Vocabulary of sounds; speculative expressions/modals
Level	All
Time	15–30 minutes
Preparation	Make a sound recording of several different types of music, e.g. African drums, Indian sitar, Caribbean steel band or calypso, heavy metal, Indonesian gamelan, etc. Make or buy a recording (if possible) of sounds from everyday life, e.g. water gushing from a tap, water draining down a sink, chopping wood, hammering metal, knives and forks clattering on a plate, etc.

Procedure

1 Students work in groups of four. Explain that you will play a tape of some music (or sounds). After students hear the tape, they should think of how they could mime what they hear. Play the tape. Students make notes on their planned mimes.

2 Play the tape again. Students then rehearse their mime for each item, using their notes if necessary.

3 Play the tape a third time. This time, each group performs its mime as the tape is playing.

4 Play the tape a fourth time. This time, two groups join up and perform their mimes for each other. They then discuss what they did.

Note

In steps 1–4 above, students may decide either to mime the actual action which produces the sound or the music, or perform body movements which 'interpret' the music in ways they feel match it.

See also 6.13 Pictures from music.

3.11 Normal, slow, fast

Aim	To use mime as a stimulus for detailed observation and description
Focus	Past tense narrative; language of sequencing: *first*, *next*, *after that*, etc.
Level	All
Time	30–40 minutes
Preparation	If using the examples in Box 7, make enough copies so that each group has one.

Procedure

1 Students work in groups of four or five. Give each group 15 minutes to prepare and rehearse a short mime of an incident – if possible, a humorous one. You can either tell students the story, or give them a copy to work with. Box 7 provides three examples.

2 Tell students that they have a few more minutes to prepare their mime sequence. They will do it once at normal speed, once in slow motion, and once speeded up (like a silent movie – fast and jerky).

3 Each group joins with another group and performs the sequence at the three different speeds. The group observing has to describe precisely the sequence of actions they have observed. Every group will both perform and describe.

4 Conduct a whole-class feedback on the activity.

Notes

1 As well as being very funny to watch, the slow-motion and speeded up mimes force the group performing to make all three mimes accurate and precise. The three versions also allow the observing group more time to register the sequence of actions.

2 If you have access to video, it is worth filming some of the mimes. You can use these both as feedback and as a way of introducing the activity with other classes.

3 Rather than doing the mimes at different speeds, ask students to do them to reflect a given mood word: *happily*, *sadly*, *aggressively*, *energetically*, *lethargically*, etc.

See also 1.15 Slow motion, 3.3 Metronome mime.

Box 7

Student 1 is chewing gum. He takes it out of his mouth, sticks it on a park bench and leaves. Student 2 comes along and sits on the bench. Finding the gum stuck to her trousers, she pulls it off, rolls it into a ball and throws it on the ground. She leaves. Student 3 comes along and steps on it. She angrily peels it off her shoe and sticks it on a lamppost, then leaves. Student 4 comes along, puts his hand on the lamppost for support while he adjusts his shoe. Finding the gum on his hand, he sticks it back on the park bench, and walks away. Student 1 comes back to the bench, finds the gum, picks it up and puts it back in his mouth and starts chewing again.

Five people are standing in a queue at a bus stop. A bus appears in the distance. They all turn heads and watch it approach. It does not stop but goes speeding by. This happens three times. Each time they get more agitated. Another bus appears in the distance. This time, one person lies down in the road to stop it. It does not stop! The others carry the body away.
(A less gruesome ending is: The bus stops. Everyone rushes to get on. Then the bus does not move. It has broken down. Everyone has to get off and join the queue again.)

An old tramp is lying on a park bench. He is very dirty. A businessman comes along. He squeezes himself on to the end of the bench near the tramp's feet. Then a lady with shopping bags comes along. She squeezes on the end of the bench and the businessman taps the tramp on the shoulder to make room. Then a young man and his girlfriend come along. They squeeze on next to the woman with the shopping. By now, the tramp has been pushed to the far end of the bench. He cannot lie down, so he cannot sleep. He is angry. Suddenly, he gets an idea. He starts to scratch his head, then under his armpits, then his arms, then his legs. The businessman also starts to scratch, and so does the woman, and so do the young couple. Suddenly, they all look at each other in horror, get up and walk away from the bench. The tramp smiles and lies down to sleep again.

3.12 Hotel receptionist

Aim	To activate students' vocabulary and syntactic knowledge through the detailed interpretation of a piece of mime
Focus	Vocabulary input can be adjusted to group level and purpose; question forms; speculative expressions/modals
Level	All
Time	30 minutes plus
Preparation	Write out about ten sentences on separate slips of paper. These will all relate to possible inquiries a guest might make to a hotel receptionist. Box 8 provides some examples which can be copied.

Procedure

1 Students work in groups of eight to ten. Explain that, in each group, one student will play the role of the hotel receptionist, and another will be a guest. The guest is completely unable to speak, so must convey everything by mime. The guest will have a slip of paper with a message on it. This must not be shown to anyone else in the group. In the first stage, the object is to convey the essence of the message to the hotel receptionist (and the group). In the second stage, the receptionist (with the help of the group) must identify the precise words which make up the message.

2 Students sit in a semi-circle behind the hotel receptionist, who faces the guest (see diagram). Distribute a different slip to each group, and the miming begins. Although the hotel receptionist is the main questioner/interpreter, anyone in the group can chip in with suggestions.

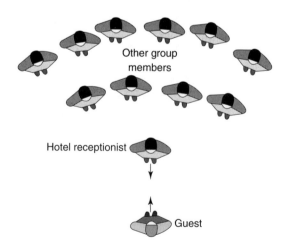

Other group
members

Hotel receptionist

Guest

Box 8

Elementary or Lower-Intermediate

Can I leave a message for Mr Fish, please?

_____

My key doesn't work.

_____

I need a doctor, please.

_____

Can you change some Euros (or other currency) for me?

_____

How can I get to the airport?

Intermediate

Do you know where I can buy a good umbrella?

_____

Can you tell me what time it is in Beijing now?

_____

My mother is arriving tomorrow. Can you send a car to meet her at the airport?

_____

There is a strange man asleep in my bed. Please do something!

_____

How do I get to the famous Bong Tombs?

_____

Advanced

Do you give a discount for large family groups?

_____

When I opened my cupboard door, I found a corpse hanging inside.

_____

Is there a doctor in the hotel? I think I may have food poisoning.

_____

Excuse me, but when I went to my room just now, I found a snake in the bed.

_____

Can you help me? I locked my passport and air ticket in my room safe last night. Now I've forgotten the combination.

_____

3 When a group finishes before the others, simply give another slip to a different guest, change receptionists, and continue.

Notes

1 It is important to insist on the two-stage process. It is relatively easy to work out the gist of the message but retrieving the precise wording requires students to really work on all the possible word combinations they have available. It is as if they run through a mental card index, thus recycling and reactivating as much language as they have in their heads.

2 The activity is an extremely rich one, and keeps the students' attention fully engaged. Even those who do not speak are silently or sub-vocally trying out language which might fit.

3 This is an activity worth repeating as a regular feature of your course. You can easily tailor the messages to the language items you have recently taught, or wish to revise. And the messages can reflect the language level of your class.

See also 3.1 What am I doing?, 3.4 Difficulty with large or small objects.

4 Working with the voice

The human voice is a wonderful instrument, and it obviously plays a critical role in communication. The more clearly and expressively we speak, the more effectively we convey our messages. What we say is often less important than the way we say it.

The voice is also a badge of identity, and an infallible indicator of mood and attitude. In a very real sense, we are what we speak, and others make judgements based on the way we sound. If we are uncertain of ourselves, our voices will 'tell on' us. If we are tired, our voices will betray that fact. If we are in a bad mood, our voices will let it be known!

We can, however, work on our voices to strengthen them and to make them more sensitive instruments of communication. Voicework can help build confidence in our ability to express ourselves in a clear, vibrant, natural voice. And this is surely an important part of being able to use a foreign language (or even our own) well.

Some people are fortunate in having a naturally good voice, but for most of us, it can only be acquired through hard work. The good news for language learners is that they get a double benefit: acquiring good voice habits while acquiring the foreign language.

The activities in this chapter apply to language learning some of the very wide range of techniques which actors use. For those interested in going further into this field, there are references to some books on voice at the end of the book.

Preparing for voicework

In this section we shall suggest some physical activities for relaxation and warming up. Our voices work better when we are in a state of relaxed alertness and are physically 'centred'. If we are tense or 'off-centre', this will have a negative effect on our voices. These activities also offer valuable opportunities for reinforcing vocabulary (especially related to parts of the body and movement) and for practice in listening comprehension through the repetition of instructions.

4.1 Relaxation

Procedure

Standing relaxation
See instructions for Activity 1.17.

Semi-supine
1   If you have a suitable surface, or even exercise mats, ask students to lie
    down as in the illustration. They should have their knees raised and feet
    flat on the floor, forming a triangle with the floor. They may use a book or
    pillow to support their head. They should feel their back gradually
    spreading on the floor.

2   Play some music softly (Baroque or New Age music is best). Tell students
    simply to breathe slowly, with eyes closed, and to visualise their body one
    part at a time, starting at the crown of their head and working down
    towards their toes. There is no need for them to do anything except
    visualise. The relaxation will happen without forcing it!

Shoulder lifting
The shoulders and neck are one of the main sites of muscular tension in the
body. Unless they are relaxed, breathing is inhibited and this has a knock-on
effect on voice quality and power.
1   Students work in pairs. They face each other. One student takes hold of
    the upper arms of their partner, just below the shoulders. They then lift
    their partner's shoulders, and let them drop back into place. It is
    important that the one whose shoulders are being lifted allows this to
    happen, and neither tries to resist it, nor tries to 'help' by raising their
    own shoulders. Students then change places. This simple exercise has the
    effect of leaving the shoulders in a 'normal' relaxed position.
2   If there are cultural taboos on touching, students can do the activity
    alone, by raising their shoulders as high as possible, and then letting go.
    This is, however, less effective than the pairwork.

Shoulder and head rolling

Students stand. They roll first the right shoulder, then the left. Five rolls toward the front, and five rolls toward the back on each shoulder.

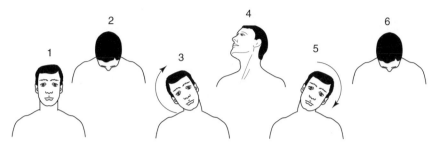

For the head rolls, students should start by letting the head drop forward so that the chin rests on the upper chest. Then, very slowly, and without straining, they bring the head up towards the right, as far back as is comfortable and back round to the starting position, all in a smooth rolling motion (see illustration above). It may help them to visualise their head as resting on a ball bearing at the base of the skull. They should do five head rolls to the right and five to the left.

See also 1.13 Feeling your muscles, 1.16 Just relax, 1.17 Directed relaxation.

4.2 Physical warm ups

Procedure

Pushing up the sky

Students stand in the balanced position. They raise their right arm with the palm facing upwards (see illustration at the top of page 72). They take a deep breath. As they release the breath, they push their hand upwards as far as possible in a series of short movements. It may help if they visualise themselves pushing up the sky. They do this five times with the right arm and five with the left.

This exercise has the effect of stretching the muscles along the sides of the body, and opening up the area between the bottom of the ribcage and the hip bone. This is the area we breathe into.

Rocking and rolling your pelvis

Students stand in the balanced position. They slowly rock their pelvis from side to side by shifting the weight from one leg to the other (see illustration 1). They do this five times, then come back to the balanced position. They then rock their pelvis from front to rear – again five times (see illustration 2).

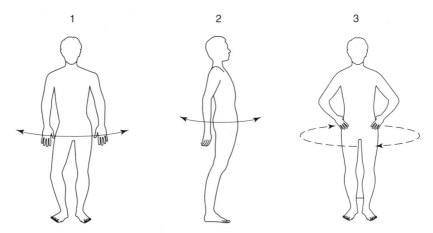

Finally, they stand in the balanced position with hands resting lightly on their hips. As they breathe in, they roll their pelvis to the right, then breathe out as they return to the starting position. They do five rolls to the right and five to the left. It is important that only the pelvis moves, not the shoulders and head (see illustration 3).

The base of the spine is another site of tension which needs to be relaxed and warmed up if we are to be centred and ready to breathe well.

The diver

Students take up a position as if they were preparing to dive into a pool: knees slightly bent, arms stretched out in front. As they breathe in, they lean forwards and throw their arms backwards. They then breathe out, bringing their arms back to the front again (see illustration). They do this five times, then return to the balanced standing position.

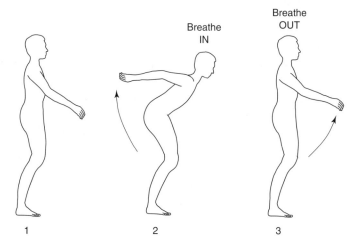

Breathe
IN

Breathe
OUT

1   2   3

See also 1.14 From seed to plant.

4.3 Breathing

In order to use our voices well, we need plenty of air to support them. Breathing is something we all do, yet many people take only shallow breaths into the upper chest. This kind of breathing may seem 'normal' but it does not support a strong sustained use of the voice.

Procedure

Give yourself a hug

Students stand in the balanced position. They hug themselves tightly by putting their left hand round the right shoulder and the right hand under the left armpit. Holding themselves as tightly as possible, they take a deep in breath, then release slowly. They do this five times. Then another five times with right arm on left shoulder and left hand under right armpit.

In this position, the bottom of the back is being held open, making it easier to breathe more deeply.

FRONT

BACK

The great conductor

Students visualise themselves as a great orchestral conductor. They stand in the balanced position. They breathe in deeply as they raise arms to shoulder height, wide apart. They look to the right and the left to show the orchestra they are ready to begin. They breathe out slowly. Suddenly, someone in the audience gets a call on their mobile phone! They drop their hands to their sides in a gesture of annoyance, and at the same time take a very deep breath.

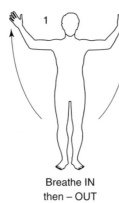

Breathe IN
then – OUT

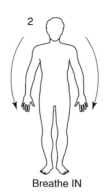

Breathe IN

Blowing out candles

Students visualise a row of twelve candles in front of them. They take a deep breath and blow out all the candles one by one. This means they have enough breath in reserve for the last one! For students who are not too old(!), they can visualise a number of candles corresponding to their age.

The car tyre

Students visualise a car tyre. First, they have to pump it up by taking very short breaths and making short *pfff, pfff, pfff* sounds as they inflate the tyre. Then they visualise it as having a puncture: they take a very deep breath and release the breath as slowly as possible on a long *PFFFFFFF* sound.

See also 1.11 Breathing.

4.4 Warming up the voice

Just as athletes need to warm up the body, actors need to warm up their voices. All of the following activities are useful for this purpose. They should all be approached with an attitude of fun. Students usually enjoy them a great deal.

Procedure

Bouncing the sound

Students stand in the balanced position. They then flop over from the waist so that their head and upper body is hanging loosely down. They then unwind slowly on an in breath till they are standing erect again. Once they are standing erect, they release a touch of sound *huh*, then again *huh*, from as deep inside as possible. It may help if students visualise the sound bouncing off their diaphragm. If they place a hand lightly on their middle, they should feel the movement when they make the sound.

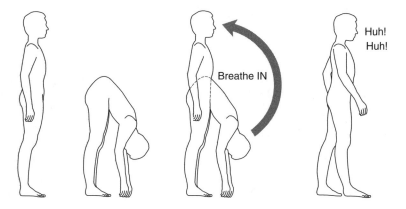

Humming into your palms

Students stand in the balanced position. They raise their arms level with their shoulders to the side, with palms upwards. They then take a deep breath and start to hum on a very low note. They should visualise the sound waves running from their centre into their hands. Continue for at least two minutes. After a time, most people do indeed start to feel a faint vibration in their palms.

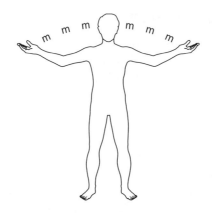

Mouth and nose

Students hum vigorously till their lips start to vibrate, perhaps even tickling. Then ask them to add a vowel to the end on the *mmmmmm* of their humming, e.g. *mmmmmmmah, mmmmmmmee, mmmmmmmoo, mmmmmmmoy, mmmmmmmeh*, etc. Repeat the process starting with a *nnnnnnn* sound, where the sound comes out of the nose. Again, students play with adding vowels. Finally, let them try *nnnnnnnnngg*, adding vowels to that too.

Slipping and sliding

1 Students pretend to be a cat making a *miaow* sound. They start very high in their voice range and slowly slide down on the out breath. They should do this as slowly as possible, making a smooth curve of sound with no breaks. They do this several times.
2 Divide students into two equal groups, which face each other from different ends of the room. They imagine they are on opposite sides of a valley and are calling to one of their friends on the other side. After a deep breath, they call *Hi!* to a student at the other end of the room. They start very high and slide down the scale till they reach the bottom.

3 Standing in the balanced position, students let their head fall back as far as is comfortable, so that their face is parallel with the ceiling. They take a deep breath, then imagine they are spraying the ceiling with sound as they make the sound *aaaaaah*, starting at the top of their voice and ending at the bottom. They do this several times.

See also Chapter 11, *Warming up.*

4.5 Preparing the articulators

Procedure

Various

A rapid run through some of these exercises will ensure that the organs of articulation – tongue, lips, jaws, soft palate and throat – are ready to go.

1 Face muscles: students make exaggerated grimaces, clench their face as small as possible, then stretch it as far as possible.
2 Jaws: students make exaggerated chewing movements of the jaw. They gently use the first three fingers of each hand to massage from the jaw joint (just below the ear), moving down with circular movements to the chin.
3 Lips: students push their lips forward as far as possible in a pout, then spread them as wide as possible in an exaggerated smile. They then expel air through the lips in a *brrrrrrr* sound. Then with a voiceless *prrrrrr.*
4 Tongue: students stick their tongue out as far as possible, then curl it back until the tip is touching the soft palate. Repeat this five times.
5 Soft palate and throat: ask students to yawn – a really big yawn. Then let them yawn while keeping the lips tightly shut. This opens up the throat aperture, which is where the sound has to come out. Students then release air from their throat by flapping open the soft palate with the sound *khaaaa*. Let them try reversing this by drawing air in on the same *khaaaa* sound. They should feel the small explosion of air each time it passes the soft palate.

ABC

1 Students sit in a circle facing outwards. One student starts by saying *A.* The one on his right says *B*, the next one *C*, and so on round the circle. They should keep up a fast pace. Run through the alphabet once in this way.
2 Then tell students that every alternate letter will be spoken loudly, every other letter very softly, e.g. *A* (very loud), *B* (very soft), etc.

3   This time, every alternate letter will be spoken on a very high note, the others on a very low note, e.g. *A* (very high), *B* (very low), etc.

4   This time, every alternate letter will be long and drawn out, the others short and clipped, e.g. *A* (very long), *B* (very short).

5   When students have got the idea with letters, give each student one word, and repeat the process. This works even better when the words are from the same sentence, e.g. for a group of ten, you might use this sentence: *Nobody sitting here knows how old our teacher's dog is.*

6   The same activity can also be done using numbers, days of the week, months of the year, colours, parts of the body, etc.

4.6   Volume

Here are just three ideas for developing (and controlling) volume.

Procedure

Voice arrow
Divide students into two equal groups, standing at opposite ends of the room (the bigger the room, the better). Tell students to visualise their voice as an arrow which makes a curve in the air before falling to its target. Give a word, e.g. *No, Tomorrow, Friday*, and tell them to shoot their word high so that it hits someone at the other end of the room.

Crescendo
1   Students work in groups of three. Each group has a different sentence (or line from a play). Students take it in turns to speak their sentence, starting very softly and building up to very loud by the end, e.g.:

It is not that I care about you, but I do care about our mother.

2   Students then reverse the process, starting very loud and fading away to very soft.

3   If you prefer, let students work in the same way with short texts (see 9.1 Mini-texts for possible texts).

Off the wall
This activity is best done in a large hall or outdoors. Students have a line or sentence to speak. They stand one metre away from a wall, and speak their line. They then move back a metre and speak it again. They continue to do this till they are ten metres or more away from the wall. In order for their

voice to reach the wall, they must increase volume progressively as they move farther away.

Working with the voice

In this section we offer a range of activities to develop confidence in using the voice, and to extend vocal range and expressivity.

4.7 Thinking about my voice

Aim	To raise students' awareness of how they sound, and other aspects of the way they use their voices
Focus	Vocabulary to describe voice quality: *high*, *low*, *sweet*, *clear*, *rough*, etc.; language of discussion: expression of opinion, agreement/ disagreement, etc.
Level	Intermediate and above
Time	One class hour
Preparation	Every student will need a copy of the questionnaire in Box 9.

Procedure

1 Students work in groups of three. Distribute copies of the questionnaire – one per student. Allow up to 15 minutes for students to complete it.
2 Students then compare their answers in their groups. They note down items where they seem to agree, and any especially interesting answers.
3 In a whole-class session, collect feedback on the questionnaires. Encourage discussion on the answers to each question. How much agreement was there? How many unusual facts emerged?

Follow-on

Encourage students to bring recordings of some of their favourite English voices for a future class.

Notes

1 We take our voice very much for granted. This activity is not itself drama but it helps students become more conscious of how they use their voices. This is a necessary preliminary to developing or changing the voice.
2 The questionnaire usually leads to lively discussion, especially question 13.

Box 9   Me and my voice[1]

1 How many different ways have I listened to my own voice?
   - in my own head, when I speak?
   - on my answering machine?
   - on a tape or video recording?
   - as an echo?
   - as a 'silent' voice in my head when I am thinking?
   - any others? ....

2 Do I usually speak fast or slow in my own language?
   ....

3 What times do I speak faster, and when slower?
   ....

4 Do I speak faster or slower than others in my family?
   ....

5 Do I usually speak loudly or softly?
   ....

6 What makes me speak louder? Or more softly?
   ....

7 When I speak English, do I change my normal speed or how loudly I speak?
   ....

8 Does my voice change when I speak English? How?
   ....

9 Do I change my voice when I speak on the phone?
   ....

10 Does my voice sound different at different times of the day?
   ....

11 Has anyone ever commented on the way I sound when I speak? What did they say?
   ....

12 Has my voice changed since I was younger? How?
   ....

13 Who is my favourite voice (actor, singer, friend, etc.)? What do I like about their voice?
   ....

© CAMBRIDGE UNIVERSITY PRESS 2005

---

[1] Adapted from *The Language Teacher's Voice* (Maley, 2000), based on an original idea by Mario Rinvolucri.

4.8 Changing voices

Aim	To give practice in changing voice quality
Focus	Pairs of opposites: *old–young*, etc.; vocabulary associated with voice quality; expressions of evaluation: *sounded very convincing, wasn't much like ...,* etc.
Level	All
Time	One class hour
Preparation	Write on the board or make copies of the material in Boxes 10 and 11.

Procedure

1   Remind students that our voices change to reflect our age and our mood. Tell them that they are actors preparing to read some lines at an audition (when an actor reads to be selected by the director to act in a play). Distribute the copies of Box 10, or ask them to look at the board. Also give out the copies of Box 11. Demonstrate the first pair of opposite adjectives in Box 10 with one of the sentences in Box 11 by speaking the sentence as an old or young person.

2   Students work in groups of four. Each group must select four pairs of opposites from Box 10, and one sentence from Box 11 to work with. They then practise speaking their sentence as indicated by the adjectives they have chosen. Everyone in the group should participate. Allow ten minutes for this.

3   Call the class back together. Group members take turns to demonstrate how they would read their sentence for each of the pairs of adjectives they have chosen – but they do not tell the class which pairs they have chosen. The class has to guess which adjectives from the way the sentence is spoken.

Notes

1   The activity focuses attention on how we vary our voices to reflect our moods. Students also come to realise that they can artificially create these moods (in English), which can be a good preparation for dramatisation.

2   With elementary level students, it may be preferable to offer just a few pairs of adjectives (*old–young, happy–sad,* etc.) and some simpler sentences. Box 12 provides some examples.

Box 10

old ------- young
friendly ------- unfriendly
kind ------- unkind
interesting ------- boring
intelligent ------- stupid
confident ------- nervous
happy ------- sad
calm ------- angry
tired ------- energetic
optimistic ------- pessimistic

Box 11

It's time to go. Let's hurry.
How much farther is it?
That was a lovely meal.
There's lots of work to do.
How often do you come here?
Have you known her for long?
I can't stand it any more.

People are funny sometimes.
There's nothing I can do to help.
Why didn't you come?
I don't understand you sometimes.
Why should I help you now?
Actually, I never liked him.
You mean so much to me.

Box 12

I like ice cream.
It's raining.
My name is …
I live in …
I can't do it.

Have you seen my friend?
What's the time, please?
Excuse me, can you help me?
Can I go home now?
Why are you laughing?

4.9 Delayed repetition

Aim	To give students time to process language before asking them to repeat it
Focus	Will depend on the texts chosen
Level	All
Time	10 minutes minimum
Preparation	Choose a short text which you want students to work with or use the example in Box 13.

Procedure

1 Read the text aloud to the class, as expressively as you can. Tell students just to listen. Then read the text again.

2 Explain that you will read the text in short sections. After each section you will pause. When you pause, students should continue to 'hear' the words in their 'mind's ear' (you should pause for about five seconds each time).

3 Read the text again. This time, students should hold each line of words in their 'mind's ear', then, when you give a signal, repeat it sub-vocally (i.e. moving their vocal organs but without making any sound).

4 Read the text again. This time, tell students to hold the line of words in their 'mind's ear', then, when you give the signal, repeat it as a whisper.

5 Read the text again. This time, after holding the line of words, students repeat it aloud.

6 Finally, if it is a very short text, read it through completely. Then ask students to repeat it from memory.

Box 13

You go.
I am left here.
How shall I pass the time –
The days, the long nights, without you?
Tell me.

AM

Notes

1 All too often we expect students to 'repeat after me' immediately. This leaves them no time to process the sounds mentally. At best we get a mechanical repetition which does not aid retention or accuracy of production. By allowing time for students to process incoming sounds on what Adrian Underhill[2] calls 'the inner workbench', they can appropriate the sounds better before uttering them. It leaves them time to pay attention to sounds before they speak them.

2 The repeated process of delayed repetitions also aids retention in memory, which is valuable both for language learning and, if you are putting on a play, for performance.

4.10 Working on words

Aim	To encourage different ways of speaking the same word
Focus	Vocabulary will depend on words chosen; work on speech parameters: speed, volume, pitch, mood, colour
Level	All
Time	20 minutes minimum
Preparation	Write on the board a list of words students have recently encountered and which you want them to learn thoroughly.

Procedure

1 Explain that students will be practising some words they have recently learnt, but in a more interesting way than usual. Give them some examples of words they have recently met in the coursebook, and how you can say them in different ways (see step 3).

2 Students work in groups of three. They decide on three of the words on the board, one each. Allow five minutes for this.

3 Students work on speaking each of their words in the following ways (you may need to write these on the board to remind them):
   • as fast, then as slowly, as possible
   • changing the intonation: rising, falling, rising-falling, falling-rising, etc.
   • as high then as low pitched as possible
   • as loudly then as softly as possible
   • changing the mood, e.g. from happy to disappointed, from kind to angry, etc.

   Allow about ten minutes for this.

[2] Underhill, A. (1994) *Sound Foundations*, Macmillan.

84

4   In a whole-class session, ask for volunteers to demonstrate some of the ways they spoke their words.

Variations

1   Students may also work on numbers in the same way. The numbers can be done separately, or as significant combinations of numbers, e.g. phone numbers, birth dates, etc.

2   Students can also work with very short sentences in the same way. These may be ones you supply, or ones chosen by themselves, perhaps from favourite plays or films, e.g. *I'll be back, I'll think about that tomorrow, I came back*, etc. You might also choose sentences recently used in class; or translations of something students have heard recently in their mother tongue.

Notes

1   This activity helps to develop a sensitivity to the impact which different ways of speaking a word have on its sense.

2   Playing with these different ways of speaking helps build confidence. It also aids retention. Repetition (an essential element in learning a language) is here being done in a motivated rather than a mechanical way.

See also 8.1 My favourite word, 10.1 One-word dialogues.

4.11 A vocal tapestry

Aim	To develop a vocal orchestration of words clustering around a given theme
Focus	Vocabulary will depend on the theme selected
Level	All
Time	60 minutes spread over two class sessions
Preparation	Select a number of themes, possibly drawing on those you have recently taught from the coursebook, e.g. food, holidays, the weather, crime, poverty, sport, pop music, etc. Write these on the board before the lesson starts. Photocopy the material in Box 14, enough for one between two.

Procedure

1   Explain that students will be preparing a kind of word tapestry, which they will perform later. They will have a theme to work with, and must find about 20 words associated with their theme word. Their objective is

to perform something which is really interesting to listen to, and pleasing to the ear.

2   Students work in groups of about ten. Allocate a different theme word to each group (or allow them either to choose one from the board, or to come up with one for themselves).

3   Allow ten minutes for groups to brainstorm as many words as possible associated with their theme word. Go round to check on progress in each group.

4   Distribute the handouts of Box 14, one between two students in each group. Gloss the handout if necessary. Tell students they should choose about 20 of their brainstormed words to include in their performance. They should discuss how they will organise their performance: who will speak which words, how they will speak, what effects they will use, etc. Allow ten minutes for this. Check to ensure that groups are on track.

5   Tell students that in the next class they will be given time to rehearse their vocal tapestries, and then perform them for the class.

6   In the next class, allow 20 minutes for rehearsal. Groups then take turns to perform for the rest of the class.

Box 14   Ways of orchestrating

- You can all speak together.
- One person can speak parts alone.
- Two or three can speak parts at once.
- Some people can chant the background words (maybe the theme word) while others speak individual words as 'embroidery' on this background.
- You can speak faster at some times, slower at others.
- You can speak parts loudly, others softly.
- You can speak some parts in a high voice, others in a low voice.
- You can use pauses.
- You can use special effects, like echoes, repetition, etc.
- You can add gestures and movements, and sound effects if you like.

© CAMBRIDGE UNIVERSITY PRESS 2005

Notes

1   Apart from offering opportunities for group bonding and learning to work together harmoniously (in all senses), this activity helps in recycling vocabulary in an interesting way.

2 Once students are familiar with the activity, it can be repeated at intervals, and the preparation time will be greatly reduced.

See also 4.17 Group orchestration of texts.

4.12 Shifting the stress

Aim	To practise sentence stress patterns in an interesting way
Focus	Alternative placement of sentence stress
Level	Lower-Intermediate and above
Time	20 minutes
Preparation	Make a list of about ten sentences, at the proficiency level of the students, which allow for stress to be placed at many points. Make enough copies for one per student. You can use the sentences in Box 15.

Procedure

1 Explain how stress can be moved from one word to another in a sentence, and how this can change the meaning conveyed. Demonstrate this with one of the sentences in Box 15, e.g.:
- She was buying VEGETABLES at the supermarket. (not fruit or fish or meat)
- SHE was buying vegetables at the supermarket. (not her sister)
- She was buying vegetables at the SUPERMARKET. (not at the greengrocers) etc.

2 Distribute the handout. Students work in pairs. They take turns to choose a sentence from the handout and to speak it with as many shifts of stress as possible. Their partner can challenge any stress they disagree with. (You will need to be on hand to adjudicate if necessary.) Continue for ten minutes.

3 Students change partners, and continue the activity for another five minutes.

Follow-on

With more advanced students, it may be worth discussing how stress is actually produced. Let them listen to you, or to a recording (of materials such as Bradford and Brazil's *Intonation in Context*[3]). What happens to the voice on a stressed syllable? Sometimes the pitch rises slightly, sometimes there is a slight pause or slowing down. Only rarely does it involve increased volume.

[3] Bradford, B. and Brazil, D. (1988) *Intonation in Context*, CUP.

87

Box 15

- She was buying vegetables at the supermarket.
- The film I saw on Saturday was about pirates.
- I put the car keys back in the drawer last night when I went out.
- How many e-mails did you receive from Carlos last week?
- I don't feel like kissing anyone at the moment.

© CAMBRIDGE UNIVERSITY PRESS 2005

Note

Sentence stress is one of the more difficult features to master in English, yet it can prove crucial in conveying the precise shade of meaning a speaker has in mind. Likewise, in interpreting a drama text, it is essential to get it right, so, besides offering valuable language learning practice, this activity may also be used in the early stages of familiarisation with a playscript.

4.13 Listing

Aim	To give practice in the speaking of long lists of items
Focus	Vocabulary will depend on the nature of the lists
Level	Intermediate and above
Time	20 minutes
Preparation	You may wish to provide students with lists of words clustering around possible themes, such as vehicles, vegetables, types of food, clothing, types of behaviour, personal descriptions, etc., e.g. fruit: *apples, oranges, bananas, pineapples, melons, grapes, mangoes, pears,* etc.; violent behaviour: *kicking, screaming, shouting, punching, swearing, throwing things,* etc. This is not essential, however, as you may prefer students to generate their own lists.

Procedure

1   Remind students of the intonation pattern of listing in English. There are two possibilities:
   - Each item has a rising intonation, except the last, which falls, e.g.:
     There were monkeys, lions, tigers, elephants, buffaloes, snakes, hyenas, antelopes, hippopotamuses, and crocodiles.
   - It is also possible to have a falling tone on each stressed syllable with the last one bearing greater stress, e.g.:
     He was stupid, obstinate, self-destructive, bloody-minded and rude.

2   Students work in groups of four. Assign each group a theme word (*fruit*, *birds*, *sports*, etc.). Alternatively, let groups choose a theme. Each student in the group individually makes a list of all the items which could be listed under that theme word. Allow ten minutes for this.

3   Students then compete with each other within their group, by reading their lists out as part of a long sentence. The other group members monitor their intonation. The student with the longest list wins.

4   If there is time, ask the winner from each group to read their list to the whole class. The group with the longest list is the class winner.

Variation

Do this as a class activity. One student starts with the stem and the first word in the list, e.g. *At the party we had pizza*. The next student continues, adding another item, e.g. *At the party we had pizza and Black Forest chocolate gateau* … The activity continues till no one can think of any more items. Anyone who forgets items or gets them wrong is 'out'. The winner is the student with the last item in the list.

Note

This is a practical way of revising vocabulary items along with practising listing intonation.

4.14 Elastic sentences

Aim	To help students develop breath control for longer utterances
Focus	Intonation and stress in phrasing/chunking
Level	Intermediate and above
Time	20 minutes
Preparation	Make a handout containing at least two expanding sentences. You can use the material in Box 16 for one of the sentences. Make enough copies for one per student.

Procedure

1   Distribute the handouts, one per student. Then demonstrate how the sentence can be progressively lengthened. Explain the importance of 'chunking' the sentence so that each sense group is also a tone group. Show students how pausing at the borders between sense groups can help make sense of even very long sentences.

2   Students work in pairs and take turns to speak the sentence to each other. Student A reads *Mary arrived*. Student B reads *Mary arrived late*. And so on till the end.

3 Students then move on to another partner and repeat the process with the second sentence you have provided.

Box 16

Mary arrived.

Mary arrived late.

Mary arrived late from the airport.

Mary, who had been away, arrived late from the airport.

My cousin Mary, who had been away, arrived late from the airport.

My cousin Mary, who had been away in Italy, arrived late from the airport.

My cousin Mary, who had been away in Italy visiting her boyfriend, arrived late from the airport.

My cousin Mary, who had been away in Italy visiting her boyfriend, arrived late from the airport in a snowstorm.

My cousin Mary, who had been away in Italy visiting her boyfriend, arrived late from the airport in a snowstorm just as we were getting ready.

My cousin Mary, who had been away in Italy visiting her boyfriend, arrived late last night from the airport in a snowstorm just as we were getting ready.

My cousin Mary, who had been away in Italy visiting her boyfriend, arrived late last night from the airport in a snowstorm just as we were getting ready for bed.

© CAMBRIDGE UNIVERSITY PRESS 2005

Follow-on

Once students are used to this lengthening process, they can be encouraged to use real texts which embody the same principle, e.g. the traditional rhyme *This is the house that Jack built* (see Box 17).

Variation

Rather than providing the whole set of progressively lengthening sentences, let students suggest ways in which a simple base sentence might be extended. Here are some possible base sentences: *He was happy. Jo hated carrots. Father had an unusual habit.* It is probably better, however, to do this after students have already had some experience of working with sets of lengthening sentences that you have provided, so that they are familiar with the ways in which a sentence can be lengthened.

Box 17   This is the house that Jack built

This is the malt
That lay in the house that Jack built.

This is the rat
That ate the malt
That lay in the house that Jack built.

This is the cat
That killed the rat
That ate the malt
That lay in the house that Jack built.

This is the dog
That chased the cat
That killed the rat
That ate the malt
That lay in the house that Jack built.

This is the cow with the crumpled horn
That tossed the dog
That chased the cat
That killed the rat
That ate the malt
That lay in the house that Jack built.

This is the maiden all forlorn
That milked the cow with the crumpled horn
That tossed the dog
That chased the cat
That killed the rat
That ate the malt
That lay in the house that Jack built.

This is the man all tattered and torn
That kissed the maiden all forlorn
That milked the cow with the crumpled horn
That tossed the dog
That chased the cat
That killed the rat
That ate the malt
That lay in the house that Jack built.

This is the priest all shaven and shorn
That married the man all tattered and torn
That kissed the maiden all forlorn
That milked the cow with the crumpled horn
That tossed the dog
That chased the cat
That killed the rat
That ate the malt
That lay in the house that Jack built.

This is the cock that crowed in the morn
That woke the priest all shaven and shorn
That married the man all tattered and torn
That kissed the maiden all forlorn
That milked the cow with the crumpled horn
That tossed the dog
That chased the cat
That killed the rat
That ate the malt
That lay in the house that Jack built.

This is the farmer sowing his corn
That kept the cock that crowed in the morn
That woke the priest all shaven and shorn
That married the man all tattered and torn
That kissed the maiden all forlorn
That milked the cow with the crumpled horn
That tossed the dog
That chased the cat
That killed the rat
That ate the malt
That lay in the house that Jack built.

Notes

1 Matching the 'thought length' to the physical sense group is an important skill and well worth practising regularly. By chunking the message, we make it more readily comprehensible to the hearer.

2 Regular practice of this kind also helps students internalise the typical phrase and clause patterns of English in a pleasurable way.

See also 4.17 Group orchestration of texts.

4.15 Playing with the text

Aim	To stretch students' vocal resources by speaking texts in unusual ways
Focus	Phrasing; quick verbal reflexes; anticipation; breath control
Level	Intermediate and above
Time	20 minutes at a time, spread over several lessons
Preparation	Make copies of a text for performance. This may be a poem, part of a speech from a play or an extract from a story. Box 18 provides a simple example you can use. Box 19 provides a more demanding one.

Procedure

1 Students work in groups of four. For some parts of the activity, these groups will split into pairs. Distribute the copies of the text. Read the text to students, making sure that it has been understood.

2 Suggest to students that they 'play with the text' in one of the following ways. When they finish, suggest another – and so on, until you feel they have done enough:

- In groups, one student reads up to the first punctuation mark, then the second student goes on. This continues till the end of the poem.
- In groups, students read alternate lines but only speak the vowel sounds. They repeat the activity, this time speaking only the consonant sounds. Finally, they read it normally.
- Students repeat the activity, standing. This time, when a student comes to a punctuation mark, they add a movement.
- In pairs, students read the poem speaking alternate words. They have to try to keep up a normal pace as they do this.
- In pairs, each student takes turns to read the text. In the first reading, they breathe at the end of every line. In the second reading, they breathe at the end of every two lines. In the third reading, after every three lines. If they cannot read the whole text on one breath, let them draw breath on *television* (if using the text in Box 19).

- In pairs, students take turns to read the text in the following ways. First, they speak only the first word of every line, and 'think' the rest of the line silently. Then, they 'think' the first part of each line, and only speak the last word aloud. Finally, they speak each line normally.
- In pairs, students take turns to read the text to each other. The first time, they read it in a flat, expressionless way. The second time, in an exaggerated, highly emotional way. And finally, in a normal way.
- In pairs, students take turns to read the text. They start by intoning it, like a chant. About halfway through they should slip back into a normal reading.
- In pairs, one student (without a text) stands behind another. The student in front starts to read the text (not too fast!) while the one behind tries to 'shadow' the reading. Shadowing means repeating the words spoken by the partner just a fraction of a second later.

3 After trying these activities over a lesson or two, invite students to prepare an effective group reading of the text to bring out its meaning and feeling with as much dramatic impact as possible. Suggest that they may like to draw on some of the ideas from step 2 which they have already tried out.

Notes

1 Obviously, it will not be a good idea to do all these activities in one class hour. We recommend that you try two or three of them per lesson over a period of time.
2 Though the activities may seem a little strange, they are very effective in helping students to speak the text better. By 'making strange', the texts become more easily handled when a normal reading is called for. Sportspeople often do something similar in training, e.g. swimmers may be told to swim using only one arm, or using no leg movements. This makes normal swimming seem easy by comparison.
3 By pulling the text around like this repeatedly, students rapidly become familiar with it. These activities are therefore very useful in the early stages of rehearsing a new playscript.

See also 4.17 Group orchestration of texts.

Box 18   Child's Nightmare

One is a small child, who hides on the floor.
Two is the bogey who knocks on the door.
Three are the windows that bang in the night.
Four are the pillows that hide me from sight.
Five are the fingers that grip on my arm.
Six are the prayers I say against harm.
Seven are the footsteps that thud in the hall.
Eight are the heartbeats I feel as I fall.
Nine are the hot tears that gush from my eye.
Ten is my number. I know I must die.

ALAN MALEY

Box 19   Notice

We will do our best to make your stay a pleasant one.
Please note the whereabouts of the Fire Exit.
We cannot contemplate children or animals.
Anything of value should be deposited
In safekeeping, and a receipt obtained.
Guests should not re-adjust the television.

Nothing to be prepared or consumed in the bedrooms.
Do not hang your personal laundry over the bath.
Put your ashes in the receptacles provided.

In case of illness, kindly contact the proprietor.
Please give adequate notice of your departure.
Make sure you leave nothing behind you when you go.

ELMA MITCHELL[4]

---

[4] From *Penguin Modern Poets 6* (1996) p. 99.

4.16 Listen to me!

Aim	To help students 'hold' a line or sentence even when being distracted by others
Focus	Using one's voice to get a message across against a background of noise
Level	All
Time	15 minutes maximum
Preparation	Prepare slips of paper containing sentences concerned with a need, a demand or a preoccupation. You will need five slips per group. Preferably different groups have different sentences. See the examples in Box 20.

Procedure

1 Students work in groups of six. Distribute five sentence slips to each group. Five students take a slip each. The sixth student has no slip. Let one group demonstrate how the activity works first.

2 The sixth student stands to one side a little away from the group. One of the others goes to this student and speaks what is on their slip. The sixth student has to respond. As soon as this starts, the second student goes over and interrupts using the sentence on their slip. Almost immediately, the third student joins in and tries to get the attention of the sixth student. This goes on until all five students are gathered around the sixth student, clamouring for attention to their problem or question. Make sure that everyone keeps talking. Allow just five minutes for the demonstration, then stop it.

3 Now students have seen the demonstration, let all groups start the activity. Limit it to five minutes only!

Box 20

Where's the nearest toilet?

Can anyone change a 100-euro note?

I've locked myself out of my flat. Can you help me?

I'm looking for the Manager's office.

I'm trying to get some sleep. Please move somewhere else.

Variations

1   Students work in pairs. Each student has a sentence, as above, e.g. S1 *Where is the Manager's office, please?* S2 *Why do you want to know?* The two students go on repeating their sentences in as many different ways as possible, till one of them gives up! They must use the same words every time, and just go on wrangling.

2   With more advanced students, encourage them to reformulate their message in as many different ways as possible, e.g.:

- I'm looking for the Manager's office.
- Can anyone tell me where I can find the Manager's office?
- Excuse me, where's the Manager's office?
- Do you know where the Manager's office is?

Note

The important thing is to keep talking. The ability to keep going in the foreign language, against the flow of others, will be a useful confidence booster. It will also be useful in performances involving many characters who may often speak at the same time.

See also 1.23 Gobbledy-gook.

4.17 Group orchestration of texts

Aim	To encourage ensemble work in the group performance of a text
Focus	All voice parameters; group coordination and timing
Level	Intermediate and above
Time	One class hour
Preparation	You will need one or more texts suitable for group orchestration. Make enough copies for one per student. You can use the examples in Boxes 21 and 22.

Procedure

1   Give a reading of the poem to demonstrate stress and rhythm in particular. Then explain to the class how this poem could be orchestrated by a group in various ways:

- by varying voices in terms of volume, speed or pace (including pausing), pitch level, intensity, rhythm and mood
- by varying the number of voices speaking at one time: some as solo, some with two, or three voices, some with the whole group

- by adding special effects, such as echo, overlapping lines, a background word or line repeated softly all through the performance, adding gestures or movements or sound effects.

Students' main objective will be to produce a vocal performance of the text which will be varied and interesting to listen to.

2   Students work in groups of about eight. Distribute the texts, one per student. Allow about 15 minutes for discussion and planning of how students will perform the text. You will need to monitor this carefully to make sure all groups are on track.

3   Groups then rehearse their performances at least three times, to ensure that they have a good 'flow' in their orchestration. Allow 15 minutes for this.

4   Finally, groups perform for each other.

Notes

1   The activity is excellent for developing ensemble work and group bonding.

2   The activity also provides opportunities for multiple repetition – without tedium.

3   Note that even using the same poem for all the groups, you will be amazed at how different the interpretations are.

Box 21   We Know

Monkeys are not doing it,
Snakes are not doing it,
Neither are beetles or fleas,
Lizards are not doing it,
Birds are not doing it,
They know that we need the trees,
Mice are not doing it,
Lice are not doing it,
Cats are not doing it,
Honest,
Bats are not doing it,
I know who's doing it,
Humans are killing the forest.

BENJAMIN ZEPHANIAH

© Cambridge University Press 2005

97

Box 22   Once Upon a Time

Once upon a time there lived
a small joke
in the middle of nowhere.

This small joke
was dying to share
itself with someone

but nobody came to hear
this small joke.

So this small joke told
itself to the birds

and the small birds told this small joke to the trees
and the trees told this small joke to the rivers
and the rivers told this small joke to the mountains
and the mountains told this small joke to the stars

till the whole world
started to swell with laughter

and nobody believed
it all began
with a small joke

that lived in the middle of nowhere.

Everybody kept saying
it was me
it was me.

JOHN AGARD

See also 1.18 Going with the flow, 4.11 A vocal tapestry. Many of the poems elsewhere in this book can also be used in this way.

Note that many of the activities elsewhere in this book also provide useful voicework practice, especially in Chapter 8. See 8.4. What's in a name?, 8.10 Mirror words, etc.

5 Working with objects

The world is full of objects – things we can see and touch. And language is full of words to describe objects. We live surrounded by both objects and the words that denote them. At times, objects even seem to have a life of their own, and a history, so that objects become subjects in their own right. We even hear talk of 'the tyranny of objects' – the power they have over our lives; the way they shape the way we think. They influence the way we define who we are by what we own: the car, the house, the gadgets, the clothes.

So objects are powerful things. They can influence the way we think about the world, our values and our beliefs. And, of course, the same object can take on different meanings for different people. The word/object *knife* has different connotations and associations for a butcher, a surgeon, a schoolboy, a cook or a hunter.

In terms of drama and language learning, objects offer a rich array of possibilities. They can be described; they can be used to stimulate memories, associations and the imagination; they can be transformed into symbols or icons; they can be transformed into something they are not – as when a child uses a saucepan as a helmet; and they can themselves transform us – as when we change our character by wearing a hat, a uniform or a mask. In this chapter we shall offer activities which draw on all these possibilities.

5.1 What am I holding?

Aim	To offer language practice/revision of specific vocabulary using the kinaesthetic channel
Focus	To practise question forms, and vocabulary to do with shape, size, texture, etc.
Level	Elementary–Intermediate
Time	10–20 minutes
Preparation	Bring a number of objects to class. They need to be small enough to fit into a student's hand, e.g. a paperclip, a matchbox, a safety pin. You will need at least three objects per group of six students. Here are some more suggestions: a coin, a pencil sharpener, a bottle top, a small mobile phone, a seashell, a small carved ornament, a penknife, a bus ticket, a cork, a medicine bottle, a torchlight bulb, a battery, a toothpick, a ring.

Procedure

1 Students work in groups of six. Each group stands in a circle facing inwards, with hands held cupped behind them.

2 Circulate quickly, slipping an object into the hands of one student in each group. They can feel their object, but must not look at it or show it. The group members then try, by questioning, to find out what the object is. They can only use *Yes/No* questions. They will need to learn to use these questions to narrow down the possibilities, e.g. *Is it hard? Is it made of wood? Is it smooth? Is it square? Is it heavy? Does it feel warm? Can you bend it?* etc.

3 When a group guesses correctly, take back the object, and give another one to a different student.

Follow-on

1 With Intermediate groups, you can extend the activity. When groups have correctly guessed about four objects each, they can be told that these objects were all found on the body of a murder victim. They must invent the story of how the objects are connected to the victim's death.

2 Alternatively, the objects were all in a bag found on a bus. What do the objects tell about their owner?

3 Students develop a story using all their objects, which they then act out for the class.

Notes

1 Especially with elementary level classes, you may need to give a demonstration with the whole class before proceeding with the group work. This will help remind students of the kind of questions they might ask.

2 The activity calls upon the tactile sense. In the case of the student actually holding the object, this is directly experienced. In the case of the others, it calls for a kind of tactile visualisation.

See also 5.4 The envelope.

5.2 My special object, your special object ...

Aim	To encourage careful listening and accurate retelling
Focus	Vocabulary of physical description; expressions of cause/effect (*I especially like it because ...*, etc.), appreciation (*What I like most about it is ...*, etc.); reported speech (*First you said ...*, *You mentioned something about ...*)
Level	All
Time	30–45 minutes
Preparation	For homework, ask students to think of one of their possessions they especially like. It might be a photograph, a picture, a pair of shoes, a CD, a carpet, a small figurine/sculpture, a ring, etc. Students should think about what the object is like, its appearance, and why they like it so much. They should bring it to class (if possible) and come prepared to talk about their object in English for about two minutes.

Procedure

1 Students work in groups of three. In each group, Student A will talk about their object for two minutes: what it looks like, why they like it so much. Student B will listen (taking notes if necessary). Student B then retells what Student A said. Student C has to listen carefully to Student A and then comment on the accuracy of Student B's retelling.

2 Each student has a turn in each of the three roles.

Follow-on

1 The activity can be followed up by making an exhibition of the objects (Our Favourite Things) and a written description/appreciation of them. The written descriptions would be set as a homework task.

2 If possible, find a recording and print out the lyrics of Noel Coward's famous song *These Foolish Things Remind Me of You* or Julie Andrew's *My Favourite Things* from *The Sound of Music*.

Variation

Instead of retelling, Student B can make a drawing of what Student A describes. Student C then comments on the accuracy of the drawing (assisted by Student A).

Note

If possible, students should bring in their objects to class, though this may not always be practicable. The 'show and tell' aspect always adds interest to the activity.

5.3 Metamorphosis

Aim	To develop imagination through the transformation of an object
Focus	Speculative expressions/modals: *It could be ...*, *It might be ...*, etc.
Level	All
Time	15 minutes

Procedure

1   Put an ordinary chair at the front of the room. Students work in groups of three. Each group has ten minutes to think of at least three things the chair could be or represent other than 'something to sit on', e.g. a wheelbarrow, a TV aerial, a weapon, a crown, etc. The group must also think of a way they can use the chair in a mime or sketch to show its new uses.

2   After ten minutes, each group takes it in turn to use the chair to dramatically show its new uses. They might do this through mime, or through a short sketch, or through a dramatic interview with the 'chair' (one student would have to take this role). The other groups must offer explanations, interpretations, questions and comments on what they see.

Variation

Instead of using a chair for all groups, each group is given a different object to transform, e.g. a wastepaper basket, a schoolbag, a cushion, etc. They then perform with their object for the rest of the class.

Notes

1   The ability to visualise alternative shapes and uses for an ordinary object is of course commonplace for young children. 'Let's pretend' games can be found in all cultures. Unfortunately, as we grow older, we tend to lose this ability to see things with fresh eyes. This activity is one way to restore it.

2   When groups are presenting their 'new' objects, it may be worth insisting on a fixed format, at least to start with. For example, the group presents its 'new' object and asks one of the other groups: *What do you think it is?* A group representative replies: *We think it is / could be / might be / looks like a ...* . The first group then asks: *Why do you think so? Please explain.* The other group has to come up with an explanation. The first group then asks the other groups: *Do you agree? Does anyone have a different idea?* This is one way of avoiding the tendency for groups to simply shout out one-word interpretations.

See also 5.5 The all-purpose object.

5.4 The envelope

Aim	To encourage development of the imagination by making connections between random items
Focus	Speculative expressions: *They might be, It could be, I wonder if it …* etc.; expressions of opinion, cause/effect
Level	Intermediate and above
Time	One class hour
Preparation	You need enough large manila envelopes (A4) for one per group of four.

Procedure

1 Students work in groups of four. Each group collects six to ten objects from their own pockets or bags – things like coins, keys, receipts, tickets, membership cards, etc. They have five minutes for this. They place the objects on the table in full view. They then put the objects into the envelope and exchange envelopes with another group.

2 Tell students that the objects in the envelope all belong to one person. They have to decide who this imaginary person is, what they look like, what their personality is like, where they live, what they do for a living, etc. One student acts as a secretary and takes notes. The groups have ten minutes for this.

3 Groups have ten more minutes to work out a short episode in this person's life, which involves all the objects chosen in step 1. They then decide on how to act this out in a short dramatised sketch.

4 In a small class, each group shows its objects to the class, then performs its sketch. In a larger class, each group performs for one other group.

Note

Human beings are pattern-making creatures. They look for connections between things, even where there are none. This activity takes advantage of this characteristic. The fictitious characters the students invent on the basis of the objects are often surprisingly creative and unusual!

See also 5.1 What am I holding?, 5.13 Who's the owner?

5.5 The all-purpose object

Aim	To stretch students' imagination by thinking of alternative uses for common objects
Focus	The verb *to use*: *We could use it for ...*, *It could be used for ...*, *You could ... with it ...*; clarification questions: *Is that supposed to be a coffee pot? Are those handles?*; evaluative expressions: *That doesn't look much like a net. That's a nice idea*, etc.
Level	All
Time	One class hour
Preparation	Bring in a number of common objects, enough for one object per group of five, e.g. a sock, a hairpin, a comb, a pencil, a lemon, a wire coathanger, a pair of spectacles, a fork, an elastic band, a piece of string.

Procedure

1 Students work in groups of five. Give out one object to each group.
2 Give groups ten minutes to make a list of as many uses as possible for their object, e.g. a sock could be used as a coffee filter, a mask, a gag, a fishing net, a purse for coins, a hairband, etc.
3 Each group joins with one other group. Groups take turns to give a brief explanation of all the new uses they have thought of for their object (group members take it in turns to explain one new use each). The other group then asks questions for clarification, and makes evaluative comments.
4 Each group decides which of their ideas for the object is the most creative. They then prepare a short sketch involving the reasons for using the object in this unusual way, e.g. they are out camping; they want to drink coffee but they realise they have everything except a filter; one of them suggests using a sock.
5 Each group performs its sketch for the class.

Variations

1 Instead of giving different objects to every group, give out the same object to all groups. This can then become a competition to find a use for the object which no one else has found, or to see which group has found the largest number of different uses.
2 With elementary level groups, simply ask them to find out how many things they can do with an object, e.g. with a sock: touch it, pick it up, sit on it, cut it, wear it, smell it.

Notes

1 If you have access to videos, the short *Mr Bean* films have some
  interesting ideas for improvised uses for objects. See in particular *The
  Park Bench*.
2 The activity again capitalises on the human ability to see new
  connections, to metamorphose objects into something else.

See also 5.3 Metamorphosis.

5.6 Stone, wood and metal

Aim	To encourage imaginative engagement with objects
Focus	Expression of opinion, agreement/disagreement; modals
Level	Intermediate and above
Time	One class hour
Preparation	You will need some interesting-looking, smallish stones (interesting shapes, textures, colours); some pieces of natural wood, such as dead branches, driftwood from the seashore, twigs from trees, etc. (these should not be too big); some small pieces of metal, such as screws, nails, washers, brackets, keyrings (the ring only), drawing pins, needles, etc. You will need enough of these three items for each student to have one of each, i.e. every student will need one stone, one piece of wood and one piece of metal. One way of minimising your own preparation is to ask students to bring their own objects – but you will still need to have a few items in reserve for those who forget or bring unsuitable items.

Procedure

1 To begin with, students sit in circles of about ten. They sit with eyes
  closed. Give each student one of the stones. They have to feel it carefully,
  and try to form a picture of what it looks like. What colour is it? What
  shape and texture is it? Where did it come from?
2 Students open their eyes and look at their stones. They compare notes
  with their neighbours in the group. How different are their stones? Were
  they surprised by the appearance of their stone when they saw it after just
  feeling it?
3 Students keep their stones, and close their eyes again. This time, give each
  one a piece of wood. Students again have to visualise what it looks like,
  where it came from, etc. They open their eyes and compare their
  impressions with their neighbours as before.

4 Finally, repeat the same process with the pieces of metal.
5 Each student now has three objects. Regroup students into groups of three. First, they discuss their objects – their impressions of them. Each group then has to choose just one stone, one piece of wood and one piece of metal. Their purpose in choosing is to select the three objects which seem to belong together, that share a common story, e.g. perhaps they were all found at a Stone Age burial ground, or they were all symbolic objects used in a secret society's rituals, or they were all owned by a historical character, or they were all dug up on the same building site, etc.
6 When groups have chosen their three objects, they spend about ten minutes developing the story which links their three objects. They then develop a short dramatised sketch based on this story.
7 Groups perform their sketches for the whole class.

Variations

1 You can, of course, use other objects, e.g. leaves (dried and pressed in a book are best – you can use them more than once), corks, pieces of fruit, potatoes, pieces of brick or tiles, old shoes, ornaments such as brooches, shells, etc.
2 Instead of using all three objects in step 5, each group chooses just one. They must then invent a mythology for their object. What is its significance? What does it symbolise? What stories and legends are associated with it?
3 As in Variation 2, but the group has to try to 'get inside' its object, to identify with it. They then collaborate to tell its life story through a brief dramatised scene.

Notes

1 In step 5, if some groups finish before others, ask them to find another three objects from among those left over, and to repeat the activity.
2 This is a very rich activity in terms of the power it has to evoke imaginative responses from the students. It is important therefore not to rush through it in a perfunctory way but to leave time for the imagination to work.

5.7 It meant a lot to me …

Aim	To encourage students to share feelings about messages which are special for them
Focus	Expressing feelings: *I was so shocked …, I hated it when …, I didn't know what to say …*, etc.
Level	All
Time	20 minutes approximately
Preparation	The week before this class, ask students to bring in a message which has special significance for them, e.g. a picture postcard, a letter, an e-mail. These could be: an appointment letter for a job, a rejection letter, a letter from the bank manager about an overdraft, an invitation, a card from someone special, a Valentine, a 'Dear John' letter (ending a love affair), a letter from the tax office, etc.

Procedure

1 Working individually, students have five minutes to make a list of the reasons why they chose this particular message-object.
2 Students form groups of four. Students take it in turns to show their message-object to the others in their group, and to explain why it is so special. The others express interest, ask questions, make evaluative comments, etc.
3 When all four students have had their turn, the group has to work out a brief dramatisation which involves at least two of their objects. Groups then perform their sketches for the whole class.

Note

This can be a very powerful activity if the message-objects brought in are truly significant to those who bring them.

See also 6.3 From my album.

5.8 Fashion show

Aim	To project some extraordinary properties into ordinary objects like clothing
Focus	Description of clothing, including colour, shape, texture, materials, purpose, etc.; terms for focusing attention: *Notice how …, See the way …, Note the special effects of …, Particularly noteworthy are the …*, etc.
Level	Lower-Intermediate and above
Time	30 minutes plus

Procedure

1 Students work in groups of five. They are given 15 minutes to prepare a fashion show for the other groups. For this, they can only use the actual clothes worn by members of the group. They may exchange clothes but they are not allowed to bring in anything special. Groups collaborate in writing the text which one member will use to present the show.

2 Each group has five minutes in which to present its fashion show for the rest of the class. Part of the class should be cleared as a 'catwalk' along which members of the group will parade as the presenter reads out the text.

3 At the end, groups vote on which was the best fashion show. The group chosen then presents its show again.

Notes

1 Remind groups that they can exploit the comic, ironic and fantastic possibilities of ordinary clothes masquerading as something extraordinary, e.g. *Please note the creative pattern of mud on the shoes, the elegantly torn jeans, the suggestive eroticism of the grease-stained collar ...,* etc.

2 You may need to revise some of the vocabulary and expressions before starting the activity. One source of expressions is clothing advertisements in magazines, e.g. *that chic, off-the-shoulder look, what the cool cats are wearing this summer,* etc.

See also 5.9 Where did you get that hat?

5.9 Where did you get that hat?

Aim	To use hats as a way of conveying a change of character/personality
Focus	Expressions of speculation: *I think ..., It looks as if ..., You could be ...,* etc.
Level	All
Time	20–30 minutes
Preparation	You need to get together a collection of many different sorts of hats (it is advisable to keep these together in a large box to use repeatedly), e.g. straw hats, bowlers, trilbies, top hats, fedoras, cowboy hats, conical Chinese peasant hats, Basque berets, deerstalkers, baseball caps, tweed caps, army caps, ladies' fashion hats, fezzes, surgical caps, turbans – as many kinds of hat as you can find. To start things off, ask students to bring in whatever items of headgear they can find at home.

Procedure

1 Invite one of the more extrovert students to come to the front of the class. Take a hat at random from the box. Ask the student to wear it and to walk up and down in the character of a person who might wear that sort of hat. The rest of the class try to interpret who the character is from the way the hat is worn, and the body language that goes with it.

2 Divide the class into groups of ten if it is a largish class, five if it is a small class. Distribute a few hats at random to each group. Group members take turns to wear the hats and to move and speak as a particular character. The others try to interpret who the character is.

3 When everyone has had a turn, the group must decide on one way of wearing their favourite hat that they think is most interesting/creative.

4 Each group then presents its hat/character to the whole class, through action and speech. The members of other groups try to interpret what they see.

Variations

1 Students work in groups of four. Distribute four different hats to each group. They spend a few minutes experimenting with the hats. They must then work out a sketch – either in mime, or with words added – which involves the four characters wearing the four hats.

2 An alternative to acting the character wearing the hat is to ask students to become the hat, and to speak 'in role' as the hat, e.g. a bowler hat: *I only work from Monday to Friday. I sometimes wish my owner would wash his hair a bit more often*, etc.

3 With more advanced groups, you might run a discussion about the power of hats and other forms of head covering. Why are they so much more powerful than other items of clothing?

Note

Hats seem to have a transformative power. The very fact of putting one on changes the way the wearer moves and behaves. An extreme example of this is the symbolic power conferred on those who wear crowns, mitres and military caps – not to speak of judges' wigs. This activity capitalises on the capacity of hats to change our behaviour.

See also 5.8 Fashion show, 5.10 Masks.

5.10 Masks

Aim	To use the transformative power of masks to tap into students' latent dramatic talents
Focus	Language of speculation/interpretation
Level	All
Time	40–50 minutes
Preparation	You will need enough masks for every student to have one. The most effective are often plain white, plastic half masks, i.e. those that cover the top half of the face only (see illustration). These can be readily purchased at theatre shops, or even in shops selling games, party hats, halloween gear, etc. An alternative kind of mask are the rubber representations of well-known public figures, or stereotypical characters. There are also the masks used in Commedia dell'Arte (Columbine, Harlequin, etc.) but these are rather expensive, as they are made of leather by traditional craftsmen. An alternative to purchasing masks is to make them yourself. In fact, this could be part of a project in the language class. One of the simplest ways to make a mask is to use cardboard picnic plates, cutting holes for the eyes and mouth, and attaching strings to tie round the head. It is also easy to make 'Zorro' type masks from stiff card. These will only cover the eyes but they are still effective (see illustration).

half mask

Zorro mask

Procedure

1 Students work in groups of five. Each group member is given a mask. The group then has 15 minutes to come up with a story around a given theme. This might be a myth, a legend, a real-life story of a tragic political or sports figure, a folk tale, an urban legend, an incident experienced by one or more of the group members, a romance, etc.

2 Once groups have decided on their story, they prepare a dramatised version of it (either in mime or with words) in which they will all wear their masks. They have 15 minutes for this.

3 When groups are ready, each group presents its mask performance for the whole class, which has to react to the performance by interpreting it, critiquing it and appreciating it.

Variation
You may prefer to assign a given story (myth, legend, anecdote, etc.) to all groups. They then develop their performances for the whole class, and compare interpretations at the end.

Note
The transformative power of masks is even greater than that of hats. Once a student has put on a mask, they literally become someone else. This is partly a result of the loss of inhibition when the face cannot be seen. This seems to free up students to speak and act in ways they otherwise would not. Another effect of masks is to exaggerate physical movements. This may be because vision is restricted, and the face cannot express emotions, so gesture takes its place.

See also 5.9 Where did you get that hat?

5.11 What am I bid?

Aim	To offer opportunities for making exaggerated claims for a particular object
Focus	Language drawing attention to visual features: *See how elegant the curve is ...*, *Notice the neat little ...*, *You can see how ...*, etc.; language of exaggerated claims/hyperbole: *You will never have such a bargain again ...*, *This is the most elegantly designed ... you will ever find ...*, *There is nothing to beat this ...*, etc.
Level	Intermediate and above
Time	30 minutes
Preparation	You should bring to class a number of very ordinary objects, e.g. a soft drinks bottle, an electric light bulb, a bottle opener, a bulldog clip, a polystyrene cup with cover, an old pencil, a used envelope, a postcard, an audio cassette, a plastic bag.

Procedure
1 Students work in groups of four. Distribute one object per group. Explain that students will be trying to sell their object at an auction. They

therefore need to prepare a written 'sales pitch' for their object. Their objective is to make their very ordinary object seem very extraordinary and desirable for the prospective buyer. Allow ten minutes for this.

2   Each group appoints one of its members as the auctioneer – the person who will describe and praise their object. They should help this person rehearse the sales pitch to make it as persuasive as possible.

3   Each group presents its object to the whole class in the most convincing way, trying to get students to bid for it. It is not enough just to read out what the group wrote down. There has to be genuine interaction between the 'auctioneers' and the rest of the class (the 'buyers'). The group which obtains the best price for its item is the winner.

Follow-on
Students may be asked to set up an exhibition of their objects, together with captions based on their auction descriptions.

Variations
1   With more advanced students, you may decide to teach them some auctioneer-talk, e.g.:

> *What am I bid for this exquisitely-crafted polystyrene cup – a unique example of late-20th century craftsmanship? Take a look at the clean lines, the bold lettering, the cool cream colour. Note the perfect fit of the lid. What am I bid for this fabulous item? Do I hear $5? $5 from the gentleman in the corner. Any advance on $5? Do I hear $8? $8 from the lady in the front row …*

If you are in an English-speaking country, you could organise a visit to a public auction so that students can hear this kind of language at first hand.

2   As an alternative to the auction scenario, you can set the scene in an antiques shop. Each group has several objects which they have inherited from a relative. They try to persuade the shop owner (a designated group member) to buy their objects by extolling their virtues in the same way as above.

Note
Once students get the idea of this activity as a send-up of everyday objects, they usually enter into the spirit of the auction. One incidental benefit is that, in order to write the exaggerated descriptions, students do actually have to look at ordinary objects with new eyes.

5.12 Symbols and icons

Aim	To develop imagination through attributing symbolic meaning to everyday objects
Focus	Vocabulary of 'signifying': *stands for, means, symbolises, shows, signifies, indicates,* etc.
Level	Upper-Intermediate–Advanced
Time	One class hour
Preparation	Bring in a number of objects with a potential to act as symbols or icons, e.g. a pair of scissors, a tropical shell, a piece of stone with an interesting colour or texture (like granite, quartz, mica-schist), a paint brush, a large dried/pressed leaf (such as a maple leaf), a rose, a wooden coathanger, a silver thimble, a pipe, a key, a padlock, a short length of steel chain, a corkscrew.

Procedure

1. Explain to the whole class what is meant by a symbol or icon, i.e. an object or design which is used to represent something else. Examples would be: the dove, which stands for peace; the Eiffel Tower, which stands for Paris; the Star of David, which stands for things Jewish; the hammer and sickle, which symbolised the Soviet Union and communism; a lighted candle with barbed wire twined round it, which signifies Amnesty International, etc. Show the class the rose you have brought in. Give them five minutes, individually, to note down what this flower symbolises for them. Students share their ideas.

2. Students then work in groups of three. Give each group one of the objects you have brought along with you. Their task is to brainstorm all the possible symbolic meanings of the object. They need ten minutes for this.

3. Groups then choose one symbolic meaning for the object. This may relate to a country, a set of beliefs, a political party, a new product on the market, an association, etc. They produce a slogan to accompany their symbolic object, plus an explanation for their choice. They should then prepare a dramatic presentation of their symbolic object. Allow 15 minutes for this.

4. Each group in turn comes to the front, shows its object and performs its dramatic presentation for the whole class, including its slogan. When a group finishes, anyone in the class can ask for further explanations, ask questions, disagree with the appropriateness of the symbol, express appreciation, etc.

Follow-on

1 If there is time, conduct a class discussion of the way symbols pervade our lives, and how they are subtly (and sometimes not so subtly) linked with products for consumption, particularly through branding (the Lacoste crocodile, etc.).

2 In this class or in a later one, students can be asked to choose or design a symbol or a logo for their class, together with a dramatised presentation.

Variation

Follow the procedure for step 1. Then tell students they are to design a new product to launch on the world market. They must decide what their product is and decide on an appropriate and striking symbol to represent it. They then proceed as in step 4.

Note

We are daily exposed to the power of symbols based on objects. Symbols are, like metaphor, so much part of our lives that we cease to notice them, or to pay attention to them. This activity offers students the opportunity to reflect on the nature of symbols, and to create some of their own.

5.13 Who's the owner?

Aim	To deduce the characteristics of a person from an object they owned
Focus	Expressions of cause-effect; modals: degrees of likelihood
Level	Intermediate and above
Time	One class hour
Preparation	Bring in a number of objects which are evocative of the uses to which they may have been put, e.g. a pair of old gardening gloves, a pair of old shoes or trainers, a wooden spoon much used in cooking, an old fountain pen, an old wallet, a pair of antique, steel-rimmed spectacles, a much-thumbed book or music score, an old pack of playing cards, a battered old hat, a much-used child's toy, an old pocket watch and chain. The main thing is that the objects should show clear signs of wear.

Procedure

1 Students work in groups of four. Give one object to each group. Allow five minutes for them to examine it carefully, noting down anything they notice about it. How old is it? What was it used for? etc.

2 Tell students that they are detectives, like Sherlock Holmes. The object has been found at the scene of a crime, or in the room of someone who is missing, or among the belongings of a person who died many years earlier. They must try to build up a picture of the person who owned the object, and what their life was like. Allow ten minutes for this.

3 Each group joins another group and takes turns to show its object, and 'present' the character they think owned it. They will need to give reasons for their decisions, e.g. *We think this watch belonged to a man. It isn't the kind of thing a woman would wear. He was probably middle-aged. About 50 perhaps. Young men don't wear this kind of watch. It's not very special or expensive-looking, so he probably was not wealthy. Maybe he worked in a bank or an office*, etc. The other group should question and probe the interpretation they are offered.

4 Each group works on the *other* group's imagined character to design a set of questions they want to ask about his/her life. One person in each group then role plays the suspect, and is questioned by the other group's members.

Follow-on

1 Following from step 4, students can be asked to develop a short scene which reveals the personality of their character.

2 Groups can be asked to prepare a dramatic monologue where the object describes its feelings and thoughts. Alternatively, the object itself can be interviewed.

Note

It is common to hear of auctions where the possessions of famous people like pop stars, film actors and other celebrities are sold. This shows a fascination with the 'aura' of objects. It is as if we believe that objects somehow acquire some of the power or qualities of their owners. The activity is an extension of this belief. It also capitalises on the fascination we all continue to have with the powers of deduction of the great Sherlock Holmes and detectives like him.

See also 5.1 What am I holding?, 5.4 The envelope.

6   Working with visuals

'A picture is better than a thousand words', goes the old saying. In language teaching and drama we could equally well say, 'A picture can stimulate a thousand words'. One of the reasons for this is that different people 'see' the same picture differently. We all interpret pictures in different ways, partly as a result of associations based on different past experiences. This is a rich resource for discussion.

Using visuals is clearly an advantage for those students with visual dominance, but it can be helpful for all students to receive inputs through more than one sensory channel. The more channels we can use, the better the chance that the information will get through and be incorporated into the pattern of existing knowledge.

Visuals, of course, do not simply mean pictures 'out there'. They also include the visualisation which takes place 'in here' – inside our own heads. Indeed, these inner visualisations in the mind's eye may be even more powerful than the ones we meet outside in the world. This is also true of pictures we ourselves draw, however poor we may consider ourselves as artists.

In this chapter, activities will be suggested which touch on description, interpretation, association and visualisation as ways in to language learning through drama.

On a practical note, it is well worth building up a collection of pictures in the various categories suggested by the activities: portraits, pictures with a lot of activity going on, pictures with two people interacting, etc. These can either be pasted on to card or laminated so that they can be used over and again as a permanent resource.

6.1 Self-portraits

Aim	To stimulate discussion of personal features
Focus	Vocabulary of personal description, especially adjective + noun phrases, e.g. *long eyelashes*, *green eyes*, *short hair*, etc.
Level	All
Time	20–30 minutes

Procedure

1 Each student draws a self-portrait in which their most characteristic feature is exaggerated as in a cartoon. Explain that this is not an activity to produce great art, but just to have fun, so it does not matter if their pictures are rudimentary. They do not show their pictures to each other.

2 Divide the class into two equal groups. Each group goes to different sides of the classroom. Collect the pictures from Group A and distribute them to Group B. Distribute Group B's pictures to Group A.

3 Each student tries to identify the person depicted on the picture they have been given. When they think they have found the person, they approach them and briefly discuss the picture. There will be some milling about because the student who does the identifying will in turn be identified by someone else. When students have found their portrait's subject, encourage them to speak with others too, comparing the drawings and the people they depict.

4 If you have a class display board, ask students to arrange an exhibition of 'Our special features', pinning up the portraits and writing their own captions, e.g *This is Marco, the boy with the biggest smile in the class.*

Follow-on

Collect the portraits at the end of the class. For the next class, make a selection of some of the more striking ones. Distribute three of these portraits to each group of four. Groups then prepare a short 'missing persons' description involving the three characters, to be read dramatically as a radio or TV 'breaking news' feature. Groups perform their broadcasts for the whole class.

Notes

1 Many students will say they cannot draw. Try to persuade them gently that no great skill or effort is needed. To show they are not alone in lacking artistic talent, draw an exaggerated portrait of yourself on the board!

2 Students are sometimes very hard on themselves, and care has to be taken, especially with adolescent groups, that some people do not become the butt of mockery. Usually, this activity tends to develop more sympathy and understanding among students, and it is a good group-solidarity activity, but you still need to keep a watchful eye for malicious taunting.

6.2 Identikit

Aim	To stimulate genuine discussion through the reconstruction of pictures
Focus	Questions: *Do you have ...?, Is there a ...?, Are there any...?*; vocabulary depends on pictures selected
Level	All
Time	20–30 minutes
Preparation	You need a set of varied pictures taken from magazines/newspapers. Cut each picture into the number of pieces corresponding to the numbers you want in each group, e.g. in a class of 24, you might decide to group students in fours – this would mean you would need six pictures, each cut into four pieces (see below).

Procedure

1 Mix up all the pieces of pictures. Distribute one each of these randomly to all the students.

2 Students circulate, trying to find a piece which fits their own picture fragment. However, they are not allowed to show their picture fragments until, through questioning, they think they have found a fit. Gradually, they will find the other pieces of their picture. They then become a group with one complete picture.

3 Each group discusses its picture in terms of who the people are, where they are, and what they are doing. They then prepare a short sketch based on their picture. They can prepare the story line in class, and write the dialogue as homework. The sketch can then be performed in a later class.

Notes

1 The activity equalises opportunity to participate, since both stronger and weaker students have fragments, and all are necessary for the completion of the activity. Also, the random distribution of fragments ensures that the groups will be mixed ability, thus preventing all the 'good' students from clubbing together.

2 If you wish to tie the activity in more closely with your syllabus or textbook, choose pictures with vocabulary related to them.

6.3 From my album

Aim	To use pictorial stimuli from students' own lives to develop a sketch
Focus	Questions: *Who? Where? What? Why?* etc.; vocabulary will depend on content of pictures
Level	All
Time	One class hour
Preparation	If possible, make a slide or OHP transparency of a photograph which means a lot to you personally. Alternatively, make copies of it (one between two students). In a previous class, ask students to bring in two photographs or pictures which mean something special to them.

Procedure

1 Bring your own chosen picture to class. Show it to the students. Ask them why they think it might be so special for you. Then discuss your reasons with them.

2   Students work in groups of four. They show each other their pictures, and explain why they are so important to them. The other group members ask further questions about each picture.

3   Each group selects one picture from each student. They then work out a story which links these four pictures and incorporates the personal significance they have for the students who brought them along. They prepare a short dramatised sketch based on this story line.

4   Groups join together and tell their story/perform their role play. They then show the pictures it was based on and ask each other questions about the significance of the pictures chosen.

Follow-on
Groups can prepare a visual display of the pictures they worked on and the written versions of the stories they developed.

Note
The fact that students are the ones who choose the visual input adds personal interest to the activity.

See also 5.7 It meant a lot to me … .

6.4   Space invaders

Aim	To create an imaginary world based on a visual input
Focus	Expression of proposals: *Let's …, I suggest we …, Why don't we …?*; reactions to proposals: *That's a good idea, I don't think that will work …*, etc.
Level	Lower-Intermediate and above
Time	One class hour
Preparation	Bring in plenty of blank sheets of A4 paper and coloured felt pens.

Procedure

1   Form groups of four. Distribute paper and pens to each group. Tell them they are going to draw some visitors from outer space who have landed on Earth. They should discuss their aliens before drawing them. What do they look like? What clothes do they wear? What is their spaceship like? Do they have any weapons or equipment? etc. Give them 20 minutes for the discussion and the drawings.

2   Groups then have ten minutes more to decide on what their home planet or star is like, what people eat, how they behave – their customs and

habits, how they communicate, their history, and above all, why they have come to Earth. They should write down what they decide.

3   Allow another ten minutes for each group to prepare a presentation they will make to humans after they land on Earth. Each person in the group must take an active part. Their objective is to reassure the humans that they are not a danger (even if they are!).

4   Each group presents its alien civilisation to the rest of the class. At this stage, the humans (the rest of the class) may ask any questions they like, or challenge the aliens.

Follow-on

1   You could use the poem in Box 23 for choral dramatisation (see 4.17 Group orchestration of texts).

2   Groups can make a display of their pictures with explanatory captions.

3   This activity can be developed into a full-scale project if there is time, and if students are sufficiently interested in it. The project would require them to research in more detail the scientific/astronomical background of the alien group, to produce artefacts from the alien culture, such as clothing, tools etc., and perhaps things like *The Daily Alien* newspaper, etc.

Variation

Instead of groups presenting their culture to the whole class, each group can work with one other group. Their objective is to present their culture to the other group and to demonstrate how they are superior to the other group.

Note

The notion of 'alien' may be linked at some point to the problems encountered in cross-cultural communication with other groups here on Earth!

Box 23

– We come in peace from the third planet.
Would you take us to your leader?
– Bawr stretter! Bawr. Bawr. Stretterbawl?
– This is a little plastic model
of the solar system, with working parts.
You are here and we are there and we
are now here with you, is this clear?
– Gawl horrop. Bawr. Abawrhannahhanna!
– Where we come from is blue and white
with brown, you see we call the brown
here 'land', the blue is 'sea', and the white
is 'clouds' over land and sea, we live
on the surface of the brown land,
all round is sea and clouds. We are 'men'.
Men come –
– Glawp men! Gawr benner menko. Menhawl!
– Men come in peace from the third planet
which we call 'earth'. We are earthmen.
Take us to your leader.
– Thmen? Thmen? Bawr. Bawrhossop.
Yuleeda tan hanna. Harrabost yuleeda.
– I am the yuleeda. You see my hands,
we carry no benner, we come in peace.
The spaceways are all stretterhawn.
– Glawn peacemen all horrabhanna tantko!
Tan come at'mstrossop. Glawp yuleeda!
– Atoms are peacegawl in our harraban.
Menbat worrabost from tan hannahanna.
– You men we know bawrhossoptant. Bawr.
We know yuleeda. Go strawg backspetter quick.
– We cantanta bawr, tantingko backspetter now!
– Banghapper now! Yes, third planet back.
Yuleeda will go back blue, white, brown
nowhanna! There is no more talk.
– Gawl han fasthapper?
– No. You must go back to your planet.
Go back in peace, take what you have gained
but quickly.
– Stretterwarra gawl, gawl …
– Of course, but nothing is ever the same,
now is it? You'll remember Mercury.

EDWIN MORGAN

6.5 High points

Aim	To develop a dramatisation from visual inputs provided by the students themselves
Focus	Past tense narrative; description of people and places; providing justifications/questioning
Level	Lower-Intermediate and above
Time	One class hour

Procedure

1 Students work in pairs. One student in each pair draws a picture of a particularly important moment in their life based on a *place*. The other student draws an important moment based on a *person*. Allow ten minutes maximum for this.

2 Students share their pictures with their partners, giving explanations about their own picture and asking questions about their partner's picture. Allow ten minutes for this, too.

3 Each pair joins another pair. They show their pictures, and again explain the incidents they relate to. This helps to consolidate the information they are sharing.

4 Each group of four develops a short improvised dramatisation using the incidents in the two places, and the two people depicted. Groups then perform this for the whole class.

Notes

1 The fact that the incidents are drawn from the personal experience of the students makes this a more motivating activity. You will need to monitor carefully in case incidents of a scary or over-personal nature are chosen.

2 You may need to gently point out that there is no need for a high degree of artistic skill.

6.6 Portraits

Aim	To develop character description based on careful observation and intuitive judgement
Focus	Vocabulary of physical description; expressions of speculation, agreement, disagreement; question forms
Level	Lower-Intermediate and above
Time	One class hour
Preparation	You will need a set of portrait photographs or pictures – one portrait per group. The focus of the pictures should be the face of the subject. Subjects should be chosen on the basis of strongly-marked characteristics. See the example in Box 24. It is better to avoid well-known public figures.

Procedure

1   Students work in groups of four. Give each group one of the portraits. Allow 15 minutes for them to discuss their picture. Their discussion should focus on the following aspects of the person portrayed:
    - How old might the person be?
    - What might his/her occupation be (or have been)?
    - Family circumstances (married or not etc.)?
    - Favourite occupations?
    - What kind of a personality?
    - Likes and dislikes?
    - Where does the person come from?
    - Life story?

    One person in each group acts as secretary and keeps notes on what is agreed.
2   When the interpretations have been agreed, each group exchanges its picture with another group. They have just five minutes to interpret the new picture – along the same lines as they did for their own picture.
3   Each group joins the group with which they exchanged pictures. They compare their interpretations of the two portraits.
4   Each group now chooses one of the two portraits. They must first agree on an interpretation (usually this will be the one the original group decided). They then speculate about what kinds of thing that person might say in real life. Remind students that most people tend to use phrases or expressions which 'label' them in some way, e.g.:

    It's a hard life.
    You can't trust anyone.

How lovely!
There's no point in worrying about it.
Things will work out somehow.
Who cares?
That's the way things are.
You never know your luck.

Students brainstorm as many phrases as possible, keeping a careful note of them. They then choose the five best expressions for their character. They practise saying these phrases in the voice they think their character might have.

5   Each group nominates a representative, who shows the portrait to the whole class and speaks out, with appropriate dramatic emphasis and expression, the phrases which their group chose as representative of their character. In other words, they must become the character they have invented. The class can ask them any questions they like, and they must reply 'in role'.

Box 24

Follow-on

1 Students can prepare a display of the portraits, with a written description and a list of the phrases they think the character might use.

2 In a later lesson, the portraits, character descriptions and phrases can be used as the basis for a dramatisation involving three of the characters.

Notes

1 We make judgements about other people partly on the basis of their physical appearance. This activity helps to activate the vocabulary and language we need for this kind of interpretation.

2 The move from character interpretation to speech is an important step. Part of our perception of another person is the things they say, and the way they say them. Developing a sense for this is important both for everyday communication and for drama work.

See also 6.7 Becoming a picture.

6.7 Becoming a picture

Aim	To develop the ability to put oneself in someone else's shoes, to take on the character of someone else
Focus	Descriptive terminology of places and people
Level	All
Time	One class hour
Preparation	You need enough pictures for one per student. The pictures should show the portrait of someone interesting to look at. Avoid portraits of well-known people.

Procedure

1 Students work individually. Give each one a portrait. Tell them that they are going to 'become' this person. Then allow 20 minutes for them to flesh out their new personality. They should make notes to remind themselves of their interpretation. Put up the guidelines in Box 25 on the board or OHT to help focus their thinking.

2 Each student joins with a partner. They show each other their pictures. Then they introduce themselves as the person in the picture. When they have finished, they can ask supplementary questions and make comments.

3 Ask for a volunteer, or nominate one student, who will be interviewed by the whole class. The student must reply to all the questions in role.

Follow-on

In the next class, students work in groups of four, and use their pictures/
characterisations to develop a dramatised sketch involving all four characters.

Note

The devil is in the detail! The more specific and detailed students' description
and interpretation is, the more convincing their new personality will be.

See also 6.6 Portraits, Chapter 11, *Improvisation* and *Rehearsal*.

Box 25

The world outside the frame of the picture
- Where was this picture taken? What can be seen outside the frame?
- What things are near? Far?
- What sort of place is this? How does it look, sound, smell?
- Are there other people nearby? What do people do here?
- Why are you (i.e. the person in the portrait) there?

The person
- Name, age, where born, (city, country), family?
- Where do you live?
- Occupation/career?
- What are you most proud of in your life?
- What do you enjoy doing most?
- How would you describe your usual appearance?
- How would you describe your personality?
- What do you hate most?
- When you leave this place, where will you go? What will you do next?
- What kinds of food do you like?
- What kind of clothes do you wear?
- How do you walk, sit, stand? What does your voice sound like?

6.8 Bringing a picture to life

Aim	To develop an interaction between two people on the basis of a picture
Focus	Language of present action, e.g. *is doing, is saying, is trying to*; vocabulary dependent on particular pictures chosen
Level	Intermediate and above
Time	One class hour
Preparation	You need one picture for every two students. The pictures should contain two people involved in some kind of interaction. See the example in Box 26. Avoid pictures with too much background detail.

Procedure

1 Students work in pairs. Distribute a different picture to each pair. Partners need to discuss their picture, decide what is going on, who the two people are, what kind of personalities they have, what their relationship is. Allow ten minutes for this.

2 Students use their information to develop a short interaction between the two people in their picture. What are they saying to each other? What is the topic? What is the outcome? They rehearse and prepare to perform their interaction. Allow 15 minutes for this.

3 Each pair joins another pair and brings its picture to life by performing it. The pair on the receiving end can raise questions and comment on the performance. How well does the interpretation they have witnessed fit their own opinion about the picture?

Follow-on
If possible, let students prepare a display of their pictures with a printed version of the dialogues they have developed below each picture.

Box 26

Variation

Carry out steps 1 and 2. Then tell students that their picture is an advertisement. They must decide what product they are advertising, and what the text of their advertising pitch will be. They then perform their advertisement for the whole class.

Notes

1 The activity leads to intense discussion both at the preparation stage and following students' performance.
2 The activity helps to develop a sense of the shape of interactions, and to promote anticipation about what others may say in given circumstances.

See also 6.7 Becoming a picture, Chapter 11, *Improvisation* and *Rehearsal*.

6.9 Picture sets

Aim	To develop a story line from a random set of pictures
Focus	Expressions of speculation, suggestion, agreement, disagreement; vocabulary specific to pictures selected; present tense/past tense narration
Level	Intermediate and above
Time	One class hour
Preparation	You will need five pictures per group. These should be arranged in sets so that there is variety within each set, e.g. a set might include a portrait, a street scene, an interaction between two people, an aeroplane and a banana. Keep some additional pictures in reserve.

Procedure

1 Students work in groups of four. Distribute one set of five pictures to each group. Allow ten minutes for them to familiarise themselves with and discuss their pictures. Help out with unknown vocabulary where necessary.
2 Each group works out a story which links all five pictures. If they wish, they can exchange one of their pictures for a picture drawn at random from the reserve pile. Allow a further 15 minutes for this.
3 Groups rehearse a dramatised version of their story and perform it for the whole class. Before they perform, they should display their pictures in the sequence they appear in the story.

Follow-on

1 Groups can prepare a display of their pictures with the story printed out below the picture sequence.

2 Alternatively, ask students, individually, to write up their stories as homework.

Notes

1 The activity invariably gives rise to much lively discussion, both within and between groups.
2 Some groups will decide to use present tense narration to make the story more vivid. Others may prefer past tense.

See also 6.10 Faces and places.

6.10 Faces and places

Aim	To develop a dramatisation on the basis of random combinations of pictures of people and incidents
Focus	Language of discussion: speculation, suggestion, agreement, disagreement, etc.; vocabulary specific to pictures selected
Level	Intermediate and above
Time	One class hour
Preparation	You will need two portraits per group of six, and one picture of a 'problem situation', e.g. a traffic jam, people crowding round an airport check-in counter, a building on fire, a flooded village, a car stopped by police for speeding, etc.

Procedure

1 Students work in groups of six. Distribute two portraits at random to each group. They discuss the portraits in as much detail as possible, trying to build a complete interpretation of the personality and background of these two characters. They should make careful notes. Allow 15 minutes for this. Then take back the portraits.
2 Now distribute one 'problem' picture to each group. Allow just five minutes for them to work out what is happening, who the protagonists are (if any), how they might be feeling, etc.
3 Tell groups that they must somehow integrate the two people whose portraits they discussed in step 1 into the problem situation. To do this, they will have to consider how these two people might behave in this situation, what roles they might play, what they might say, etc. Groups will then produce a brief dramatisation of the resulting scenario. Allow 20 minutes for this.
4 Each group presents its dramatised version to the whole class. Allow for questions and comment if there is time.

Note

As in many of the activities in this chapter, the main challenge is to make the imaginative leap to connect items which have no intrinsic connection.

See also 6.9 Picture sets, 8.14 People, places, problems and things.

6.11 Split cartoons

Aim	To use a cartoon sequence as the stimulus for a dramatised reconstruction
Focus	Expression of degrees of likelihood: *might be, could be, must be,* etc.; sequencing expressions: *first, next, after that, before that, last,* etc.; vocabulary specific to the cartoons selected
Level	Intermediate and above
Time	One class hour
Preparation	You need to copy a number of sets of a cartoon sequence. The number of sets will depend on the number of frames in the sequence, and the number of students in the class. In the example in Box 27 there are seven frames. If you had a class of 21 students, you would need three sets for the class. Each frame in the sequence should be cut out separately to allow one per student.

Procedure

1   Divide the class into groups corresponding in size to the number of frames in the cartoon sequence (see Preparation). Each student in a group is given one frame of the sequence. This is not to be shown to anyone else in the group. Allow up to ten minutes for students to study their cartoons carefully so as to be able to describe them.

2   Explain that the pictures form part of a sequence making up a complete story. Allow 15 minutes for students, in turn, to describe (not show!) their pictures to the rest of the group. They may act out, as well as simply explain, their picture. As they hear the descriptions, group members try to see where their own picture fits. They may ask supplementary questions. Gradually, a sequence will suggest itself. When this point is reached, students can lay down their frames. The group then collaborates in telling the story, frame by frame. At this stage, the group may decide to rearrange the sequence.

3   When groups have the story clear, they prepare a short dramatisation based on it. This will involve some dialogue and movement. Groups perform their dramatisations for the whole class.

Box 27

Box 27 continued

Box 27 *continued*

Variation

In a largish class, you could distribute one frame per group. Each group then sends a representative to other groups, describing its frame, and hearing the description of other groups' frames. In full class session, groups then describe their frames and try to fit the whole story together.

Note

The activity gives rise to intense discussion as students try to piece together the story. It is important that they do this verbally before the pictures are revealed.

See also 6.9 Picture sets.

6.12 Mood pictures

Aim	To use a picture with a strong mood feeling to stimulate a dramatised incident
Focus	Vocabulary of mood: *creepy, peaceful, lighthearted, oppressive, scary, exhilarating, awe-inspiring*, etc.
Level	Intermediate and above
Time	One class hour
Preparation	You will need to find reproductions of art pictures or photographs which are particularly atmospheric (see *Dancing at the Moulin de la Galette*, Renoir, in Box 28). Other possible examples might include: *The Scream* (Edvard Munch), *The Bathers at Asnieres* (Seurat), *The Enigma of Arrival* (de Chirico). Photographs which are atmospheric work equally well. You need enough pictures for one per group of four students.

Procedure

1   Students work in groups of four. Give each group a different picture. Allow ten minutes for them to discuss it in detail. What is the mood that the picture provokes? Help with vocabulary as necessary.

2   When they have decided on a predominant mood for their picture, groups work out a scenario based on the mood and the scene in their picture. This should involve four characters – one for each of the group members. Who are the characters? What are their feelings towards each other? What do they say? What happens?

3   After 20 minutes' preparation time, each group performs its dramatisation either for another group or for the whole class. This is followed by questions and discussion.

Note

The atmosphere set by a picture can prove a powerful stimulus to the imagination. The atmosphere is the backdrop: the students provide the characters and the action suggested by it.

Box 28

6.13 Pictures from music

Aim	To build up a 'gallery' of pictures stimulated by listening to music, which will form the basis for an art gallery guided tour
Focus	Language of colour, size, position; verbs of representation: *shows, represents, signifies, means*, etc.; explanatory language: *this is because ..., the reason for ... is ...*, etc.
Level	All
Time	One class hour
Preparation	You will need: four sheets of large paper (A3) and a box of markers for each group; cassette recorder and a music tape (choose any striking piece of music you like – preferably, it should not be familiar to the students).

Procedure

1 Students work in groups of four. Each group will have a large sheet of paper and access to the coloured markers. Tell them to start drawing as soon as you start the music. They can draw anything the music suggests to them. When you stop the music, they are to stop drawing.

2   Play the music for about 20 seconds. Then stop. Students now move to the right in their group, so that they take over the picture started by their neighbour. (Alternatively, students pass their papers to the person on their left, whichever is easier.)

3   Play the music for another 20 seconds or so, then stop. Students continue to draw – on the new paper. They can either extend what the first student began, or draw something completely new. Continue this process till each student gets back the paper they started with.

4   Each group now has to decide on a theme for the pictures it has drawn, e.g. they may decide that all the pictures suggest 'wind', or 'flying', or 'pain', or 'excitement', or 'magic'. They must also give each picture a title.

5   Groups display their pictures – either on the floor, the desk, or the wall. They should try to make the display as attractive as possible. They then prepare a brief presentation of their exhibition: the sort of things a curator in an art gallery might say to visitors: who the artist was (an invented person!), how and when the pictures came to be painted (imaginary, not real – everyone knows the pictures are really by the students!), the theme and how the picture titles relate to it, anything special to notice about the pictures (colours, shapes, etc.).

6   Groups take it in turn to present their exhibitions to the rest of the class. At this stage, anyone may ask questions. If it seems appropriate, the class votes for the best exhibition.

Follow-on

1   Students can be asked to write a poem or a short caption for their picture as homework.

2   If you live in a place where art exhibitions are accessible, try to arrange a class visit to one. Students may be able to collect brochures of the exhibition to look at in a subsequent class. How different is the language of the brochures from what they used in their own gallery tour?

Notes

1   This can be done at any level, though, of course, the degree of sophistication will vary according to language proficiency and cognitive maturity.

2   It is important not to allow too much time for the drawing each time you stop the music. The drawing is more spontaneous if it is done under time pressure.

6.14 Recreating the scene

Aim	To develop a dramatisation of a scene from an art picture
Focus	The dialogue/vocabulary will depend on the specifics of the picture you choose; language of discussion
Level	Upper-Intermediate–Advanced
Time	One class hour
Preparation	You need to find an art reproduction which depicts a scene with a number of characters and some fairly clear ongoing action. See *The Betrothal* in Box 29 as an example. You need enough copies for one per group of six.

Procedure

1 Students work in groups of six. Distribute one copy of the picture you have selected to each group. Allow them ten minutes to discuss it. What is going on? Who are the people in the picture? What might they be saying to each other (or to themselves)? What is going to happen next?

2 Groups develop a dramatisation of the scene in the picture. This will involve allocating roles to each of them, deciding on what the characters are saying to each other (the dialogue should be written down) and deciding on an outcome (how the scene will finish). Allow at least 20 minutes for this.

3 Groups then either perform for another group or for the whole class. This will depend on how many groups there are.

Variation
Each group can be given a different picture to dramatise.

Follow-on
If there is sufficient interest, and if the dramatisations are memorable enough, students could compile a small booklet with the picture and the different dialogue scenes they have developed. This booklet can then be used with future classes as performance texts.

Note
The picture, if well-chosen, guides the dramatisation quite closely. Having this framework means students do not have to imagine the action, so that they are free to concentrate on what they will say and how they will say it. Interestingly, groups will come up with very different dialogue versions of the picture.

See also 2.12 Picture memory, Chapter 11, *Improvisation* and *Rehearsal*.

Box 29

6.15 Guided visualisation

Aim	To develop a dramatised scene from internal visualisation
Focus	Vocabulary will depend on the nature of the scene; language of discussion
Level	Intermediate and above
Time	One class hour
Preparation	Write out a script of the scenario you will read to the students or use the examples in Boxes 30–32. Remember that you are trying to evoke sharp sensory, especially visual, impressions, so the vocabulary you use should be carefully chosen to reflect this.

Procedure

1 Explain that you are going to read a short text. While you read, everyone should keep their eyes tightly closed, and try to imagine the scene as you describe it. Tell them to try to see and feel the scene in as much detail as they can. Then read the text in a measured, calm voice, leaving plenty of pauses.

2 Students work in groups of three. They share their impressions of the scene they have just heard about. How much agreement is there? Where is this taking place? Who are these people? What do they look like? Why are they there? What will they say and do next? What will be the outcome? Allow about 15 minutes for this.

3 On the basis of what they have agreed, the three group members take the roles of the people in their text and develop a short dramatised version of what happens next. They will need about 20 minutes for this.

4 Groups join one other group and perform their dramatisation, followed by discussion and comment.

Follow-on

1 The written texts of the dramatisations produced on the basis of this single visualisation may be printed up and kept as performance texts for another class.

2 As homework, ask students to prepare a short visualisation text of their own. This can be used in a later lesson, with students reading their texts to other members of a group or to the whole class.

Note

Visualisation is one of the most powerful processes we have access to. Yet it is so often neglected in education. In this activity, it is the internal representations of an event which guide the whole dramatisation. We do not 'see' things the same in the theatre of the mind, but we can share what we do see. And this gives impetus to imaginative discussion.

See also 1.27 Directed group visualisation.

Box 30

It was such a lovely party. The dancing, the music, the flashing lights, the excitement, the fun … And Elizabeth just knew that Roy had been watching her all evening. If only … she thought. He was there now, tall, dark and handsome – but dancing with that blonde Jane again. Suddenly she felt hot and tired. The noisy band was giving her a headache. She saw some stairs and decided to get away for a while. When the next dance began, she quickly ran up the stairs. It was dark up there but she found a door, pushed it open and fell on the bed. It was so soft and cool. From downstairs, she could hear the music and the laughter. Was she in love with Roy? Suddenly she heard footsteps on the stairs. The door opened and a figure stood outlined against the light from downstairs. But it was not Roy …

Box 31

Efua could not sleep. Maybe it was the strange food she'd eaten for supper. Maybe it was the heat of the summer night. Moonlight streamed through her window. She could hear the sound of the waves breaking on the rocks below the hotel. Cicadas were trilling in the trees. She decided to take a walk down to the sea. She slipped on her cotton dress and tip-toed, barefoot, down the stairs. There was no one around. She tried to open the old wooden door quietly, but it squeaked just the same. But no one stirred. They were all fast asleep. Even the man at the reception desk was gently snoring. She stood for a moment, listening – but all she could hear was the wind, the sea, the cicadas, and her own heart beating, beating … She started to walk down the steep cliff path. The stones hurt her feet, but soon she was standing on the small beach, her feet wet with the waves. It was so beautiful: the moon reflected in the water, the sound of the waves on the rocks, the dark cliff behind her. Suddenly she felt that she had to go for a swim. She slipped off her dress and ran quickly into the waves. The water welcomed her. She swam out till she could see the lights of the nearby town. She felt totally relaxed. Slowly, she began to swim back to the beach. As she felt her feet touch the sand, she looked up. There was a dark shadow standing next to her dress …

Box 32

It was dark. He opened his eyes. At first, he could see nothing. His head hurt where they had hit him with the rifle butt. He shivered. It felt cold and damp in the place. Gradually his eyes got used to the gloom and he could make out the rough stones in the wall, glistening with wetness. He tried to move but realised his arms and legs were tied tightly to the hard, wooden bed. He moved his head to the right. On the far side of the cell he could see a small circle of light coming through a spyhole in the steel door. From somewhere in the building he could hear the echo of distant voices speaking a language he did not recognise. He turned his head to the left. There was a small window criss-crossed by bars, high in the wall, with a little moonlight coming through it. He realised that there were two other people in the cell. He strained his eyes and managed to distinguish the one nearest to him. It seemed to be a young woman. The farther bed was occupied by an enormous bulk. The man must be a giant, he thought. The man was snoring loudly. His own wrists and ankles were sore from the tight ropes that bound then to the bed. He struggled to loosen the ropes. It was then that the woman spoke. 'We don't have long,' she said.

6.16 Characters from fiction

Aim	To use character descriptions from novels and short stories to help students visualise characters and develop a dramatised scenario
Focus	Vocabulary of physical and character description; expressions of speculation, degrees of likelihood, suggestion and counter-suggestion
Level	Intermediate and above
Time	One class hour
Preparation	You will need to collect a number of short character descriptions drawn from fiction. You need a minimum of four such descriptions but the more you have, the better it will be. Try to build up a collection over time. Box 33 provides some examples.

Procedure

1 Students work in groups of four. Distribute one character description randomly to each group. Allow 15 minutes for them to read and discuss the character described in the text.

2 Groups have to imagine that they are about to interview the person in the text for a TV programme. They design a list of the questions they would like to ask. They should also discuss how the person in the picture might respond.

3   One student from each group then goes to another group. This student acts the part of the person in the picture. The group members act as interviewers on the programme and conduct the interview.

Box 33

It was true, Carter thought, eyeing his wife over the coffee cups, her slave bangles chinking in time with the coffee spoon: she had reached an age when the satisfied woman is at her most beautiful, but the lines of discontent had formed. When he looked at her neck he was reminded of how difficult it was to unstring a turkey. Is it my fault, he wondered, or hers – or was it the fault of her birth, some glandular deficiency, some inherited characteristic? It was sad how when one was young, one so often mistook signs of frigidity for a kind of distinction.

GRAHAM GREENE *The Blue Film*

The man who opened the door was sixty years old at least with snow-white hair and a pink babyish skin. He wore a mulberry velvet dinner jacket, and his glasses swung on the end of a wide black ribbon.

GRAHAM GREENE *When Greek Meets Greek*

Philip had never seen the girl, but he remembered Baines had a niece. She was thin and drawn, and she wore a white mackintosh; …

GRAHAM GREENE *The Basement Room*

He studied the woman who sat in his chair covertly; he thought he'd seen her somewhere, the mink coat, the overblown figure, the expensive dress. Her face was familiar but unnoted, like that of someone you pass every day at the same place. She was vulgar, she was cheerful, she was undoubtedly rich.

GRAHAM GREENE *Jubilee*

© CAMBRIDGE UNIVERSITY PRESS 2005

Variation

Either use the kind of short extracts as in Box 33, or choose a scene from a novel or short story involving tension between three or four characters. Students form groups of four. Each one takes the role of one character. They project themselves into the shoes of their character. Each student in the group is then interviewed by the other members of the group and must answer the questions they ask 'in role'.

Note

Working from textual descriptions in this way also stimulates visualisation. When we read, we 'see' things in our mind's eye. The fact that everyone sees things differently leads automatically to discussion as students negotiate their 'visions'.

See also 1.27 Directed group visualisation, 6.15 Guided visualisation.

7 Working with the imagination

The two previous chapters were based on drama activities stimulated by objects and visuals. In this chapter, all the activities originate in the imagination of the students. The activities need no other materials. By imagination, we do not mean vague day-dreaming or unfocused fantasising. The imaginative faculty (or 'creativity' as it is sometimes called) can be stimulated. One of the most productive ways of doing this is to ask *What if ...?* questions: *What if the world were run by children? What if people could no longer have children?* (the question P.D. James answers in her novel *The Children of Men*), *What if we redefined what counts as a crime?*, etc. So, in this chapter, students will be invited to imagine how things might be different if ..., as well as creating new things. Having created something original, they will then dramatise it.

7.1 Something in common

Aim	To use unrelated items from students' minds to prepare a dramatised scene from a documentary film
Focus	Vocabulary will depend on the items students come up with
Level	Upper-Intermediate–Advanced
Time	One class hour
Preparation	Write on the board a number of possible topics for a documentary film, e.g. Industrial safety / The health risk from smoking / Water supply problems associated with dam building / Life insurance / Scuba diving in Thailand / Dental health / Cattle ranching in Australia / The fashion industry / Trekking in the Himalayas.

Procedure

1 Ask students to note down four things: a superstition, a noisy machine they find irritating, a childhood memory, a disagreeable tic or mannerism. Allow five minutes for this.

2 Students form groups of four. Each group must choose, through discussion, just four items: one of each category in step 1. Each member of the group has to contribute one item. This should not take more than ten minutes (e.g. a group might end up with *a ladder*, *a mobile phone*, *having measles* and *teeth sucking*).

3 Groups devise a brief sequence from a documentary film on one of the topics on the board. Their sequence has to feature all four of their items chosen in step 3. Their sequence will include a commentary (read by one or more of the group members). Allow 15 minutes for them to devise their sequence.

4 Groups then take turns to act out their sequence for the others, with feedback from the class.

Notes

1 It is important in step 2 that every group member has one of their items chosen so that no one feels left out.

2 As in other activities, it is the need to make connections between previously unrelated items which stimulates the imagination.

7.2 Statues

Aim	To use live humans as statues to develop imaginative dialogue
Focus	Instructions/parts of the body: *Move your head to the right*, etc.; comparison: *look like ..., stand like ...*, etc.; description: *Here we have ..., Notice how ..., The ... is ...*
Level	Elementary and above
Time	One class hour

Procedure

1 Before students start, do a little revision of vocabulary for parts of the body, and the movement words they will need: *put, lift, raise, lower, hold, bend, straighten, take, move*, etc.

2 Students work in pairs. One is the 'sculptor', the other the 'statue'. Between them, each pair should agree about where the statue will be located (e.g. in a city square, in a concert hall or theatre, in a park, on the top of a mountain, etc.), who or what the statue represents (e.g. a war hero, a famous scientist, an actor, a writer, a musician or composer, a politician, a religious leader, etc.), what it is made of (e.g. wood, stone, metal, etc.), and whether it is representational (i.e. lifelike) or abstract. Allow up to ten minutes for this.

3 The sculptors then work on their statues, by giving instructions to the statue on how to stand or sit, the position of limbs, the way the head is to be held or turned, the gestures of the hands, the facial expression, whether the eyes are open or closed, etc. This must be done through clear instructions, with no physical contact. When the sculptor is

satisfied, the statue has to hold the position. This should take about ten minutes.

4   Each sculptor in turn gives a public speech to the whole class about the statue. This will be a very self-important speech, e.g. *What I have tried to do here is …, Notice the magnificent way …, See how I have captured the moment of his victory*, etc. Others may interrupt to ask questions or to disagree, e.g. *Why are her eyes closed? What's he pointing at?* If the class is too large, let this be done in groups.

5   Each sculptor moves to a different statue. Statues can now speak about how they feel. If they are not satisfied, they ask the new sculptor to change their position to improve the statue, e.g. A *I'm fed up with pointing at that building over there.* B *OK. Put your hand to your forehead instead.*

6   If there is time, sculptors and statues change places and repeat the activity.

Note
The stage of giving instructions offers lots of language practice. Step 3, when the statues are being praised by their makers, offers opportunities for dramatic excess.

See also 2.1 Freeze!

7.3 Amazimbi

Aim	To invent some phrases in a completely new language
Focus	Language of discussion; language for talking about language
Level	Intermediate and above
Time	One class hour

Procedure

1   Students work in groups of four. Each group is asked to invent five phrases in a completely new and unknown language. Each phrase should have a clear, demonstrable meaning. Remind students that languages have rules. Allow about ten minutes for this. Here is an example:
   Amazimbi – Sit down.
   Amazombi – Get up.
   Neikko – Yes.
   Kaiiko – No.
   Mi iizim kula? – How do you feel?
   Kula klapa hammingi – I feel great.

2   One student from each group goes to another group. This student becomes a teacher of the new language to the other group. The 'teacher' may only use gesture to teach. The 'learners' can ask questions or offer possible meanings in English. Once an utterance has been understood, it should be practised to get the correct pronunciation! Allow about 20 minutes for this stage.

3   Conduct whole-class feedback. What did students notice? What have they learned from this activity about how languages work? What was most difficult? What regularities did they discover? Each group can be asked to explain the way their language works. In the example given in step 1, *ama-* is an imperative form, *-zimbi* means *down* and *-zombi* means *up*, *kula* might have some connection with verbs of feeling, etc.

4   Students return to their groups. They prepare a rhythmic chant combining all the phrases from their new language for performance to the class (see 4.11 A vocal tapestry).

Follow-on

Students work in pairs. One student gives a short talk in gobbledy-gook (see 1.25 Gobbeldy-gook). The partner acts as an interpreter of the talk into English. Pairs circulate for ten minutes, exchanging talks/interpretations.

Notes

1   On the surface, it may seem strange to be inventing a new language when students are supposed to be learning English. The benefit comes from the intense discussion which takes place (in English we hope!), and from the insights the activity can give students into the nature of language itself.

2   Students interested in JRR Tolkien's books may find examples of invented languages there (Elvish, etc.).

3   Do not leave out the chant in step 4. It is an excellent activity for group vocal coordination and bonding.

See also 1.23 Gobbledy-gook, 4.11 A vocal tapestry.

7.4 Patent pending

Aim	To invent a socially useful appliance, tool or instrument
Focus	Vocabulary will depend on the invention chosen; language of discussion: suggestion and counter-suggestion, etc.; presentation language/sales talk: *Here we have ...*, *Notice the little lever ...*, *This will revolutionise your life*, etc.
Level	Intermediate and above
Time	One class hour
Preparation	You will need sheets of blank paper and coloured markers. Bring to class copies of a description of a recent invention, enough for one between three. Box 34 provides some real examples of recent inventions.

Procedure

1   Students will work in groups of three. Explain that they are to come up with a new invention which would improve people's lives. Give out the copies of the description to give them an idea. Allow time for them to read it.

2   Suggest that groups first come up with what the invention is and what it will do. Then let them think of the stages of the process it involves. Finally, they draw a sketch of it on the paper provided. They should label it and give it a name. Allow 15 minutes for this.

3   Conduct a brief feedback session with the whole class to check on the ideas which have come up.

4   Each group prepares a presentation of their new invention. Their objective in the presentation is to impress possible sponsors for their new product. All three group members should have a role in the presentation. The presentation should be as dramatic as possible, involving a demonstration and lots of high-powered sales language. Allow 10 minutes for this.

5   Each group presents its invention to the whole class. The class votes for the most original idea.

Notes

1   If ideas seem slow in coming, or if some groups are stuck, you could offer examples of inventions made by past classes. Here are some examples:
   • a machine for reprocessing used chewing gum into blu-tak
   • a machine for neutralising cell-phone signals in public places like restaurants, trains, cinemas, etc.

Box 34

Researchers in Mexico have invented a new type of anti-graffiti paint, Deletum 5000, which remains effective for 10 years.

In Hong Kong, Leung Wai has invented a solar-powered device called Wetsep which purifies waste water cheaply, thus providing clean drinking water for rural areas.

In Malaysia, Ken Yeang has invented a system which pipes natural sunlight into high-rise buildings, thus improving light quality and saving energy.

- A pair of scissors with very long handles to help old people, who cannot bend down, to cut their toenails.
- A gadget for getting the shells off shrimps without getting your fingers messy.

Or simply give students a suggestion of the problem to be solved, e.g.:

- What to do with the hair clippings from hairdressers' shops.
- How to make supermarket shopping easier for disabled people in wheelchairs.
- How to make original new foods, e.g. garlic ice cream.
- How to get rid of plastic litter.
- How to get rid of dust in classrooms.

2 The dramatic element in this activity is in the presentation, and students should be encouraged to be as flamboyant as possible (presidential candidates on TV offer a good model!).

See also 7.5 Making a machine.

7.5 Making a machine

Aim To involve students in discussion, physical movement and presentation of an original machine

Focus Vocabulary will depend partly on the machine chosen, but will also involve parts of the body, movement, direction, etc.; imperatives, instructions; language of discussion: suggestion and counter-suggestion, agreement, etc.; presentation language/sales talk

Level Intermediate and above

Time One class hour

Procedure

1 Do a warm-up activity in which students practise making mechanical movements using all parts of their bodies: up and down, sideways, circular movements, spirals, small rapid movements, big slow movements. These should all be done repetitively as if they are a component in a machine.

2 Form groups of eight. Each group has to make a new machine, something never before seen on earth. Every member of the group has to be a component in the machine, except one, who will direct the others and present the machine publicly at the end. Sound effects may enhance the impression the machine makes. Allow 20 minutes for groups to work out how their machine works, what its function is and what it will be called. Here are some examples:

   • a machine for extracting chlorophyll from leaves and using it to make toothpaste

   • a machine for collecting broken glass, melting it down and making windows from it

   • a machine for compressing used tin cans and processing them into coloured wire

   • a machine for transforming old car tyres into garden furniture.

3 Circulate among groups to ensure that they are 'on task'. As you do so, tell the 'directors' to prepare to present the machine at a big trade fair. The presentation will explain what the machine is called, what it is for, how it works, and what its advantages are. The group may also want to come up with a slogan they can chant during the presentation.

4 Each group demonstrates its machine to the others, while the director gives the presentation. Anyone may ask questions after each presentation. The class votes for the best machine.

Notes

1 This activity generates great excitement and involvement. It integrates physical activity, thinking and language in a unique way. The challenge posed by the activity seems to stimulate group creativity, and the results are nearly always spectacular. If you can video-record some of the presentations, these can be used in later classes.

2 It is also a valuable group-bonding activity, which becomes part of the class history as a group, as it becomes a 'storied class' (see Ruth Wajnryb's book *Stories* in the *Cambridge Handbooks for Language Teachers* series).

See also 7.4 Patent pending.

7.6 Waking dream

Aim	To develop a group story through free association
Focus	Past tense narrative
Level	Intermediate and above
Time	One class hour

Procedure

1 Students sit or lie (if you have a carpeted surface) in a circle, facing outwards so that no one is looking at anyone else. If you have a bigger class, let students form circles of about ten students. If you can, play some quiet, soothing music (e.g. *Ma Vlast* by Smetana, *L'après-midi d'un faune* by Debussy, Indian flute music played by Hariprasad Chaurasia, etc.). As the activity gets under way, gradually lower the volume of the music.

2 Explain to students that you will begin to tell a story. When you stop, anyone can add one or more sentences to continue the story. No one is obliged to say anything. Students should only speak if and when they feel they can add something interesting to the story. Here are three story starters:

   • It was a very hot night, and the mosquitoes were biting. Outside the tent, we could hear the jackals calling, and the occasional roar of a tiger ...

   • My uncle Harry was a strange man. He loved horses, and used to carry a roll of banknotes in his jacket pocket, 'just in case I see a horse I want to buy'. He hated everything to do with the government. One day, he tore up a letter from the tax office without even opening it. 'Won't you get into trouble?' I asked him. I was only 12 at the time ...

   • Lakshmi was only 17 years old, and very beautiful. Her father was a big local landlord. Ravi was 18, and fell in love with Lakshmi the first time he saw her. There was only one problem ...

3 Let the story go on for about ten minutes. Then raise the volume of the music again and ask students to return to their normal positions.

4 Run a short feedback session, going back over the story so far. Students make notes.

5 Students work in groups of four to prepare a dramatised version of the story, which they then present to the whole class.

Notes

1 The first part of this activity is a valuable 'cooling down' activity if you want to restore calm after more hectic or more concentrated activities.

2 You need to trust that your students will come up with ideas for continuing the story. Generally, they do, though there may be some uncomfortable (for you) silences. Do not forget that silence may indicate intense thinking, so do not be afraid of silence. If it goes on for too long, one tactic is to go back to the start of the story again.

3 Once students have had a successful experience of making a story in this way, they are usually happy to do it again in a later class.

See also 1.27 Directed group visualisation, 6.13 Pictures from music, 6.15 Guided visualisation.

7.7 Festival

Aim	To develop a dramatised festival based on an invented culture
Focus	Vocabulary will depend on the type of festival chosen; modals of permission: *can/can't, must/mustn't, have to, should/shouldn't*; language of explanation/justification: *We do this because we believe ..., We keep the lid on the pot, otherwise the spirits will escape ...*, etc.
Level	Intermediate and above
Time	At least one class hour
Preparation	If you can, bring in some coffee-table books with pictures of festivals from different parts of the world. You could also set students a websearch (as homework in a previous class) for information on festivals such as Divali, Chinese New Year, Loy Kratong, Obon, Homowo, Songkran, etc.

Procedure

1 Conduct a brief class discussion about the kinds of events human cultures celebrate: religious (Buddha's Birthday, Eid El Fitr, Christmas, Hanukkah, etc.), the earth cycle (New Year, Midsummer, Harvest Festival, Rice Planting, etc.), human life cycle (births, funerals, marriages, coming of age, birthdays, etc.). Remind students that these cultural festivals usually involve special objects, certain rituals, perhaps some taboos and a differentiation of roles (male/female, old/young, etc.) Different cultures do things differently.

2 Students work in groups of six. Explain that they are going to invent a new culture and choose one special festival celebrated in that culture. They should decide on:
- three special objects which are essential to their festival
- one item of clothing used in the festival

- one special ritual (which should involve some use of language – as a prayer, a chant, a song, etc.)
- one taboo (something which must not be done – like walking on a particular spot)
- how the roles of men and women differ in the festival.

Allow 20 minutes for this.

3 Check with each group that they have come to agreement on their festival and how it is conducted. Then ask all groups to prepare a brief presentation of their festival. This can be either an explanation, or a demonstration (or both). Allow ten minutes for preparation.

4 Groups present their festivals to the class. Any student may ask questions, demand explanations, etc. If there is insufficient time in this class, carry over the presentations to the next class.

Notes

1 Students become very involved in this activity and show remarkable ingenuity in the items they choose to include.

2 Apart from its value as a language learning activity involving drama, there is a broader educational objective, namely to raise awareness of cultural differences, promote understanding that many behavioural differences are culturally determined, and develop a degree of tolerance for other cultures.

3 For those with an interest in literature, the development of a culture with its own rituals can be found in *Lord of the Flies* by William Golding (1954).

See also 5.12 Symbols and icons, 6.4 Space invaders, 7.3 Amazimbi.

7.8 It's against the law

Aim	To develop a courtroom drama based on an invented new law
Focus	Vocabulary will depend on the nature of the law in question, but some general legal vocabulary: *accuse, guilty, innocent, charge, crime, forbid, illegal*, etc.; language of discussion: suggestion, counter-suggestion, agreement, etc.
Level	Upper-Intermediate–Advanced
Time	At least one class hour

Procedure

1 Hold a brief discussion with students about laws. Who makes laws? Are laws always fair to everyone? Is there a law in their country which is particularly unpopular? Is 'law' the same thing as 'justice'? You may also

wish to refer to any popular TV courtroom dramas accessible locally, e.g. *Law and Order.* Draw attention to some of the more usual expressions used in courtrooms, e.g. *Objection! Objection overruled / Objection sustained. Did you, or did you not ...? I put it to you that ...,* etc.

2 Students work in groups of four. Ask them to imagine that they are living in a state some time in the future. They have to devise and draft one of the laws in this futuristic state. They can exercise as much fantasy as they like at this stage. Some ideas which have come up with groups include: a law forbidding the consumption of any uncooked food; a law which punishes anyone who does not spend the whole of their salary each month; a law forbidding anyone to walk anywhere outside their home; a law which makes reading books illegal (see *Fahrenheit 451* by Ray Bradbury [1953] for a novel on this subject); a law which makes it a crime to speak English! Allow ten minutes for this.

3 Hold a whole-class feedback session so that everyone can hear the ideas of the others. Encourage students to offer further suggestions at this stage.

4 Each group now has to draft its law, i.e. write it down briefly and clearly. Groups then work out a courtroom scene where the prisoner is accused of breaking this law. They need to agree on what actually happened, where it happened, who witnessed it and whether there are any extenuating circumstances. One student plays the prisoner, another the judge, another the lawyer for the defence, and another the lawyer for the prosecution. The scene should follow this outline:
   - Judge reads the accusation: *On the 4th April ... you ...,* etc.
   - Defence lawyer makes the case for the defence.
   - Prosecution lawyer makes the case for the prosecution.
   - Both lawyers ask the prisoner questions to try to establish guilt or innocence.
   - Judge sums up and directs the jury.
   Allow 20 minutes for this.

5 Groups perform their courtroom dramas. The class votes on the best one, if this seems appropriate.

Follow-on
The activity can lead naturally into a debate on the motion: *Laws are made by man. Justice is done by God.* The debate can be set up formally, with a proposer for and against and a seconder for and against. These students all

give brief speeches for and against the motion. Then discussion takes place and a vote is held. Alternative motions could include:

There is one law for the rich, and another for the poor.
Laws are there to protect authority, not to promote justice.
Judges wear wigs to conceal the fact that there is nothing underneath them.
It is no accident that 'lawyer' almost rhymes with 'liar'.

Notes

1 Apart from its value as a language learning activity using drama, the wider educational issue of law and justice is highlighted. This may help raise awareness of the arbitrary nature of laws and the need to debate unjust laws.

2 In most legal systems there is a special variety of language used by the legal profession. Do not worry about this. It is not necessary for students to learn the legal register of English to do this activity (and anyway, the court case takes place in the remote future!).

See also 7.10 Our new constitution.

7.9 Time's arrow

Aim	To develop a dramatic scene which is played backwards in time
Focus	Vocabulary for parts of the body, movement and spatial position; imperatives, instructions; language of discussion: suggestion, counter-suggestion, agreement, etc.
Level	All
Time	One class hour
Preparation	If possible, bring in a short video clip of a scene involving several people moving around. You will also need a video camera and a blank tape for recording.

Procedure

1 If you have brought in a video clip, play it (one minute is enough). Then play it using 'rewind', so that everything in the clip happens in reverse sequence – and faster than normal speed. Explain that the activity they are going to do will involve them in 'rewinding' their scene.

2 Students work in groups of five. In each group, there will be a director and four actors. They have to devise a very short scene involving action among the four actors (e.g. three people are arguing; a fourth comes up to them and tries to calm them down; they turn on this actor and chase him away). They should add words to their scene. Allow ten minutes for this.

3   Groups have to work out how to play their scene in reverse. To do this, they will need to think first of reversing the sequence of events, then of reversing the detailed physical movements each actor makes. The director is in charge of making sure that they reverse accurately, by giving instructions where necessary. They can reverse the language simply by imitating the chittering sound such scenes always make. Allow 15 minutes for them to rehearse this.

4   Groups perform their scenes both forwards and backwards for the rest of the class. If possible, make a video tape of the performances for use with other classes in future. The class votes on the scene which had the most accurate 'rewind'.

Notes

1   This activity focuses on the physical movements made, and provokes lively discussion about the difficulties experienced in reversing movements accurately.

2   The role of the director is important, so you may have to nominate who is to take this role in each group, to make sure they have the necessary language proficiency to do it properly.

3   For those interested in literature, there is an excellent example of time reversal in Martin Amis' (1992) novel *Time's Arrow*.

See also 1.15 Slow motion, 3.11 Normal, slow, fast.

7.10 Our new constitution

Aim	To invent a constitution for a country run by birds, and present it publicly in a speech
Focus	Use of *shall* to denote legal force: *All citizens over the age of ten shall have the right to vote*, etc.; vocabulary to do with rights and responsibilities; language of discussion: suggestion, counter-suggestion, agreement, etc.
Level	Upper-Intermediate–Advanced
Time	One class hour
Preparation	Make copies of Maslow's Hierarchy of Human Needs in Box 35. It may also be helpful to have copies of the US Constitution (see http://www.house.gov/Constitution/Constitution.html) and the German Constitution (see http://www.psr.keele.ac.uk/docs/german.htm).

Procedure

1 Conduct a brief class discussion about the role a constitution has in defining a country and what it stands for. If you have access to the US or German Constitutions, check out the kinds of things they cover. Let students also see a copy of Maslow's Hierarchy of Human Needs. Which of these levels of need does a constitution usually cater to? (Physiological needs? Safety needs? Love needs? Esteem needs ? Self-actualisation needs?)

2 Students work in groups of four. Each group will design a constitution – but for a country run by birds, not people! The constitution should make provisions in each of the levels of Maslow's Hierarchy. Allow ten minutes for students to note down some of the major points they will include in their Constitution for Birdland, e.g. Will it be a monarchy, a republic, a dictatorship? etc.

3 Conduct a whole-class feedback session, collecting ideas and recording them on the board.

4 Back in groups, students put the final touches to their Constitution for Birdland. They also work out a brief presentation, in the form of a speech, which will introduce their new constitution at the United Nations. Allow 15 minutes for this.

5 Each group appoints one member to make its speech to the rest of the class.

Variation

Instead of birds, the constitution could be written for a republic of computerised robots or a republic of children.

Notes

1 This is a demanding activity and can only be done with mature students.

2 By shifting the perspective from a human to a bird perspective, the issues facing those who try to draw up constitutions are made clearer. What is good for birds becomes the primary focus, rather than what is good for people. Students usually get to grips with this quite quickly and produce interesting constitutional articles as a result.

3 Those with literary interests will recall the republic (later dictatorship) of the animals in George Orwell's (1954) *Animal Farm*. Part IV of *Gulliver's Travels: A Voyage to the Country of the Houyhnhnms* by Jonathan Swift (1726) describes a republic of horses.

4 Like some of the other activities in this chapter, this activity has wider educational implications.

See also 7.8 It's against the law.

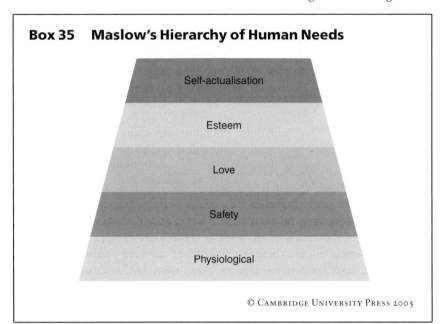

Box 35   Maslow's Hierarchy of Human Needs

Self-actualisation

Esteem

Love

Safety

Physiological

© CAMBRIDGE UNIVERSITY PRESS 2005

8 Working from/into words, phrases, sentences

We live in a web of words. They are everywhere. Without them we cannot communicate fully even our basic meanings, let alone the finer distinctions in our thinking. Words are at the heart of our first clumsy attempts to communicate in an unfamiliar language. To be 'lost for words' is to be lost indeed!

Words are not things, and yet they are. They are both more, and less, than what they seem. We combine and recombine them to achieve a multiplicity of effects: to describe, to persuade, to deceive, to curse, to love, to grieve, to light up our imagination, to bring aesthetic pleasure, etc. They are the stuff of magic. They give us power over things, and people. They afford infinite pleasure when we play games with them. As our experiences of life multiply, so the associations of the words with those experiences become more complex – so that meanings become personal as well as public. The words we use and the way we use them are subtly interwoven with our personalities.

In this chapter we shall focus on the rich storehouse of words to develop activities for communication and for dramatic effect.

8.1 My favourite word

Aim	To encourage students to personalise their relationship with words through dramatic presentation of them
Focus	Expression of likes, preferences; justification/reasons for likes/preferences
Level	All
Time	30 minutes–one class hour

Procedure

1   Tell the class about some of the words you especially like in English and why you like them. It may be that you like their sound, or the way they seem to 'fit' their meanings, or because you like the things they describe, e.g. *scrumptious* seems to me to bring together a whole complex of associations with the physical delights of some kinds of food – and it is

lovely to say; similarly, *grotty* seems to sum up all the dirty, unwashed, unpleasant physical qualities associated with sordid neglect (*sordid* is another nice word too!).

2 Ask students to think about all the words they know in English and to choose just one word they especially like. They should also have a reason for liking this word. When they have chosen their word, they should practise a way of saying it which really brings out the essential quality of the word and their affection for it. Allow 15 minutes for this.

3 Students work in groups of five and present their words dramatically to each other, together with their reasons for liking their words.

4 Each group makes a joint presentation to the whole class.

Follow-on

1 For homework, ask students to prepare to present five more words they especially like (or dislike) for a later class.

2 In a later class, students can be asked to make a selection of their words, which they compile into a chant for choral performance (see Chapter 4 Working with the voice).

Note

We recall vocabulary in various ways, but it is generally agreed that we retain words more easily if we have established an affective personal relationship with them. This activity is one way of reinforcing this bond.

8.2 The feel of words

Aim	To encourage students to form sensory links with words they know and meet
Focus	Vocabulary of sensation applied to words: *feel*, *smell*, *taste*, etc.; expressions of personal opinion: *I think* …, *For me* …, *What I feel is* …, etc.
Level	Intermediate and above
Time	One class hour
Preparation	You will need a list of about 20 nouns and verbs (see the example in Box 36). Prepare enough copies for one between two students.

Procedure

1 Explain to students that words have an effect on us beyond their literal meaning. We can perceive them as having physical properties like hard/soft, sharp/round, heavy/light, etc. In fact, for native speakers of a language, there is a remarkable degree of agreement on such judgements.

2 Distribute the list of words to pairs of students. They should choose five words. For each word, they have to decide if it feels:
   - hard or soft
   - heavy or light
   - smooth or angular (sharp)
   - dark or bright.

   Allow ten minutes for this.

3 Each pair joins another pair, and they compare notes. They then have to choose one word each from those they have discussed, and work out a way of speaking that word dramatically so as to convey their perceptions of it in terms of the four pairs of qualities above. Allow ten minutes for them to rehearse their words together.

4 Each group of four performs its four words for the rest of the class. How much agreement is there about the judgements made and the appropriateness of the way the feelings of the words were conveyed?

Box 36

Split	Grapple
Tree	Gravel
Stone	Label
Treacle	Elbow
Soap	Navel
Climb	Towel
Finger	Plaster
Grain	Muscle
Topple	Harbour
Plain	Handle

© CAMBRIDGE UNIVERSITY PRESS 2005

Follow-on

In a later class, ask students, in groups of six, to prepare a dramatised performance of the poem in Box 37.

Box 37

Some words are happy and others are sad.
Some words are scented and others smell bad.
Some words feel heavy, while others feel light.
Some words bring darkness, while others are bright.
Some words are honest and others are sly.
Some words are slimy and others are dry.
Some words are cold and some words are hot.
Some words sound tender and others do not.
Some words are untidy but others are neat.
Some words are bitter and others taste sweet.
Some words feel smooth, while others feel rough.
Some words sound dainty, while others sound tough.
Some words move quickly, some words move slow.
Some words are shrinking, while some others grow.
Some words we use little, and some quite a lot.
Some words are remembered, and others – forgot.

ALAN MALEY

© CAMBRIDGE UNIVERSITY PRESS 2005

Note

Asking students to assign physical qualities to words may seem a little fanciful, but it does help them forge additional links with these words, and thus aids retention of vocabulary.

8.3 Real English or not?

Aim	To develop a feel for the Englishness of English words through a creative drama activity
Focus	Expressions of opinion; degrees of probability; agreement/ disagreement
Level	Intermediate and above
Time	One class hour
Preparation	Prepare a set of unusual words on cards, some of which are real words, and some of which are not, e.g. these words could be English words but in fact are not: *dowlish, pylonitis, gramble*; by contrast, these words, though unlikely-looking, are real: *quark, mimsy, prang*. You will need about twice as many word cards as there are students in the class. Box 38 gives some examples to get you started.

163

Box 38

Real			Invented	
blog	lurgy		pringle	grimp
fink	primp		frutcheon	cottle
lop	splurge		grift	brishly
bloater	duffer		scrat	slive
dub	blarney		darbious	futigular

© CAMBRIDGE UNIVERSITY PRESS 2005

Procedure

1 Conduct a short discussion about English words. How do we know if a word is English or not? From the way it sounds? The way it is spelt? How do we tell the difference between a noun, a verb, an adjective, an adverb? How important is context in helping us to understand a word's meaning? etc.

2 Distribute one card to each student at random. Students should not show their cards to each other. Allow them five minutes to decide if their word is a real English word or an invented word. They should also decide what part of speech it is and how it is pronounced.

3 Conduct some class feedback on just a few of the words, writing them on the board with their part of speech and the guess about whether or not they are real English words.

4 Students work on their words again. This time allow them ten minutes to make up two sentences which will show their meaning, e.g. *He didn't sound very polite to me; in fact he spoke very brishly to me.*

5 Students circulate for about five minutes, speaking their sentences in an appropriately expressive way to others.

6 Conduct whole-class feedback, using some of the more inventive sentences produced by students. Select one or two words and try to elicit a definition from the students.

Follow-on

1 As homework, ask students to check out which of the words were really English words. Allocate five words per student, making sure they include both real and invented words. Feed back on this in the next class.

2 If there is sufficient interest, extend the discussion of words. How do we know a word is likely to be English? How do we know a word 'sounds foreign'? (e.g. Which of these sounds closest to English: *mbali*, *cszentimaszita*, *scubular*?)

Note

Apart from being a creative challenge, this activity helps focus students' attention on the Englishness of English words, and on the largely arbitrary way that meanings are assigned to sound combinations (within a set of phonological rules).

See also 7.3 Amazimbi, 8.1 My favourite word, 8.2 The feel of words.

8.4 What's in a name?

Aim	To develop rhythmical chants on the basis of proper names
Focus	Naming: personal names, place names, animal names, food names, etc.
Level	All
Time	One class hour
Preparation	As resources, it may be useful to have available: an atlas, a telephone directory (if you are working in an English-speaking country), a recipe book, a reference book of given names, such as *The Guiness Book of Names*, an encyclopedia, one of the 'Best CD' guides, etc., a list of websites where information about names can be found.

Procedure

1 Decide on one area of names you would like students to focus on: their own names, geographical names, food and drink names, animal names, names of famous people, names in 'cult' films (such as *Lord of the Rings*, *Harry Potter*, etc.). Working individually, each student makes a list of names in that category. Allow ten minutes for this. Students may need to consult reference books or websites for this step. If you think this will be necessary, set it as a homework task to save time in class.

2   Students work in groups of three. Allow 20 minutes for them to compare their lists of names and compile a rhythmic chant based on the names they have found. Here is an example based on food:

Sandwiches and omelettes,
Curries and stews,
Pot roasts and barbecues –
Which will you choose?

Students rehearse their chants. Encourage them to present their chants dramatically, varying speed, volume, pitch and intonation, etc. and adding gesture and sound effects, as in 4.11 A vocal tapestry.

3   Each group performs its chant for the whole class.

Note

Names are powerful, even magical, things. A good way to start using this activity is to ask everyone in the class for their name (or preferred nickname) and to say something about it. The class then goes on to make a chant built from all their names. This can be very empowering for everyone: to have your name recognised is a form of affirmation which can do wonders for self-confidence. It also helps to consolidate the class as a learning group.

See also 4.11 A vocal tapestry.

8.5 Words and movement

Aim	To combine words with specific movements
Focus	Will depend on specific words/texts chosen
Level	Lower-Intermediate and above
Time	30 minutes approximately
Preparation	Depending on the level, you will need to prepare lists of words, phrases or whole utterances. Box 39 provides some examples.

Procedure

1   Explain that in life, as in drama, we often accompany our speech with movement. The students will therefore be asked to perform a simple movement when they speak the words (or phrases, etc.). Demonstrate this yourself to make it clear to them. Take a single word, like *Silence!* Speak it aloud and at the same time, take one or two paces forward (or in any other direction). Repeat this, but adding a hand gesture. Finally do it again, adding a particular facial expression.

2 Write on the board five or more of the words (or phrases, etc.) from Box 39.
3 Students work in pairs, using the five words you have written on the board. They decide which of their word/movement combinations are most effective.
4 Finally, each pair presents its chosen items to the rest of the class.

Box 39

Words	Phrases	Complete utterances
Silence!	Over here, please.	Oh, it's all such a mess.
Wait.	Oh, for goodness sake!	Do you remember me? I was your mother's best friend.
Now?	Take your time.	
Who?	So that's it.	I could never take him back …
Lunch.	It's teatime …	I was eighteen when my hair started to fall out.
Babies.	That'll do.	

Variation

Start with single words. Then ask students to add a word or phrase to it as they move, e.g.:

Now? – Now do you mean? (Or: Do you mean now?)
Lunch. – Lunch is over there.

Notes

1 All too often, what we say in the foreign language is stiff and static. This activity is a way of breaking out of this straitjacket. It is also a way of integrating the language into the whole self. Language is physical. Let's keep it that way.
2 Even with advanced students, it is as well to start with single words, then move on to longer stretches of language. Theatre students are often taught to match the thought-length of an utterance to breathing and a movement.

3   This activity is also a good way into a rehearsal of a play or sketch for performance (see Chapter 11 Performance).

See also Chapter 11, *Improvisation* and *Rehearsal*.

8.6 Tableaux

Aim	To develop a complex still mime from the stimulus of a single word and its associations
Focus	This will depend on the specific theme words chosen; language of discussion and evaluation
Level	Intermediate and above
Time	One class hour
Preparation	Decide on a number of 'theme' words, e.g. *anticipation, disappointment, doubt, anxiety, satisfaction, trust,* etc.

Procedure

1   Write one of the theme words on the board. Students work in groups of six. They are going to prepare a silent, living sculpture (involving all six group members) which represents the theme word. Allow ten minutes for them to discuss ideas in groups.

2   Allow another ten minutes for groups to actually form their tableaux. When everyone is ready, groups take turns to present their tableaux to the whole class. They should explain how it represents the theme word. Other students may question them.

Variation

Rather than giving a single theme word for the whole class, let each group choose a different word. Their words may be linked to a given theme, e.g. a colour, a personal quality, an emotion, a profession, a type of weather, etc. At the presentation stage, the rest of the class would then have to try to guess what the theme word is, before commenting on the tableaux.

Note

This activity really helps students get to grips with words in a very physical sense; and, having done the activity, the words become forever associated with the tableaux.

8.7 Praise songs

Aim	To generate some chants in praise of the qualities of the group
Focus	Practice in positive adjective, noun and verb forms
Level	All
Time	One class hour
Preparation	You will need to write on the board some lists of positive adjectives, nouns and verbs as examples for step 1 of the activity, e.g. adjectives: *cheerful, helpful, happy, humorous*; nouns: *workers, team, dancers, actors*; verbs: *to joke, to assist, to cooperate, to create.*

Procedure

1   Explain what a 'praise song' is – a kind of chant which is usually recited to celebrate a person or thing. Tell students that they will be creating a praise song for their class. In it, they will use adjectives, nouns and verbs to build up a very positive picture of their class group.

2   Divide the class into three groups. Group A will brainstorm adjectives, Group B nouns, and Group C verbs. They can use the ones you have written on the board but they should find as many new ones as they can. Allow about ten minutes for this.

3   Groups report back, and you list their suggestions in the three columns on the board. Then show students how they can generate lines (sentences) on the following pattern:

   We're a cheerful team who love to joke.
   We're happy actors who love to perform. etc.

4   Students return to their groups. Allow them 15 minutes to write a minimum of five lines on the above pattern, using the words in the columns on the board (or new ones if they think of more as they work).

5   In whole-class feedback, collect the suggested lines. The class votes for the best ten lines. Write these on an OHP so that everyone can copy them down.

6   Each group spends ten minutes rehearsing how they will perform the class praise song. Groups then perform for the whole class.

Note

This is a highly motivating activity and helps with group bonding and solidarity. Students get a real kick out of celebrating their own group identity.

See also 1.8 Beat out that rhythm, 1.18 Going with the flow, 4.11 A vocal tapestry.

8.8 Group story

Aim	To use random vocabulary items to generate a narrative
Focus	Vocabulary will be randomly selected, therefore unpredictable; language of discussion and evaluation
Level	Intermediate and above
Time	One class hour
Preparation	Make sure everyone in class has access to a monolingual learner's dictionary.

Procedure

1 Students work in groups of four. Each group needs at least one copy of a reputable monolingual learner's dictionary. Demonstrate how to find a random word, e.g. you take the dictionary; open it at any page; find the first entry (on the right-hand page) of the word class you are looking for (noun, verb or adjective/adverb). Do this three times: once for each word class. Now you will have three words.

2 Tell students to open their dictionaries randomly at any page. They look for the first entry which is a noun on the right-hand page. They write this down. Then tell them to repeat the process. This time it is the first verb (i.e. full verb, not an auxiliary) on the right-hand page which they are looking for. Finally they repeat the process, this time looking for the first adjective or adverb on the right-hand page. Each group now has three words: a noun, a verb and an adjective (or adverb).

3 Students use their three words to generate a story which can be acted out – either in mime or with a script. Allow 20 minutes for this.

4 Each group acts out its story for the whole class. The class comments and asks questions to identify the words which the dramatisation was based on.

Variation

1 With lower-level classes, you can provide lists of words for them to choose from, randomly, rather than using the random dictionary procedure.

2 Students work with any good learner's dictionary. Ask them to call out any number between 1 and 738 (if you are using the *Cambridge Learner's Dictionary*). Open the dictionary at that page, say 251. Then ask students for any number between 1 and 20. If the number is 12, go to the twelfth entry on the page (if the word is a function word, go on to the next content word). In the *CLD*, the word is *fireman*. Write the word on the board. Repeat the process till you have five words listed on the board.

Students then work in groups of three. Allow them 20 minutes to work out a story line based on the five random words. One student from each group then moves to the next group and tells the story they have developed. After discussion, the host group then tells its story to the visiting student.

Note
The very fact that students are working from minimal material encourages a highly imaginative and often unexpected outcome.

See also 8.9 Off the cuff.

8.9 Off the cuff

Aim	To encourage students to speak in an impromptu situation
Focus	Vocabulary will depend on the words which crop up
Level	Intermediate and above
Time	20 minutes approximately
Preparation	Select a number of nouns and write them on separate cards or slips of paper. These may be words you want students to revise, or they may be slightly unusual words, such as *Anaconda, Lotus, Pulpit*, etc. (in this case, students must be allowed a few minutes to consult a dictionary before starting). You need enough cards for every student to have one.

Procedure

1 Students work in pairs. Distribute the cards, one per student. Students should not look at the cards yet. When you give the word to start, one student in each pair looks at their card and immediately starts to address the word on the card as if it were a partner in a conversation, but without actually mentioning the word itself. After two minutes, they stop and the partner has to guess what the word is. Here is a possible example for the word *flame*.

> *How warm you make me feel. And how useful you are: I can light my cigarette from you. I can cook my food with you. You make my pot boil on the fire. I love your red and yellow colour.* etc.

2 The second student in each pair repeats the process with the word on their card.

3 Students now write down a word of their own choice on a slip of paper. Collect the slips and redistribute them at random. Students again form pairs and repeat the process in steps 1 and 2.

Variation

Each student writes down a single noun on a slip of paper. Collect the slips of paper, mix them up and redistribute them at random. Students then work in pairs. They start up a conversation and must try to find a way of introducing their word into it naturally. If their partner successfully identifies the hidden word, they have lost.

Note

If vocabulary is to be learned, we need to provide multiple opportunities for recycling it, so that items are met in a variety of contexts and become part of the personal language world of the learner. This activity suggests one way of doing this.

See also 8.8 Group story.

8.10 Mirror words

Aim	To develop a chant on the basis of words which mirror each other, e.g. *tip–pit*
Focus	Vocabulary based on mirror words (see below); language of discussion and evaluation
Level	Intermediate and above
Time	One class hour
Preparation	You need cards containing up to ten words which have a mirror equivalent. Box 40 provides some of the more common pairs based on this principle. Notice that some are precise (sound and spelling) mirrors; some are sound mirrors only; some are spelling (but not sound) pairs. On the cards, you only write one half of the pair. e.g. *lips* (*spill* is not written). You need enough cards for one per group of four.

Procedure

1 Spend a few minutes demonstrating to the class how many words in English have a 'mirror' partner. Write up three examples on the board, e.g. *tool* (*loot*), *kiss* (*sick*), *trap* (*part*). Make sure students get the idea clearly.

2 Students work in groups of four. Give each group a card containing the ten words you have prepared. Allow ten minutes for groups to find the mirror partners of these ten words. Check the results with the whole class.

3 Groups try to put each pair of words into a sentence, e.g. *After the accident he had **nicks** in his **skin**.*

4 Students exchange their ten sentences with another group. Each group then composes a chant using at least five of the ten sentences. At this stage, they can change or improve on the sentences they have received from the other group if they wish.

5 Groups perform their chants for the rest of the class or for another group.

Box 40

Precise fit	Sound only	Spelling (not sound)
dog–god	eyes–sigh	strap–parts
top–pot	name–mane	trap–part
tops–spot	make–came	ram–mar
stab–bats	card–dark	not–ton
pool–loop	side–dice	rail–liar
ten–net	lean–kneel	live–evil
arena–an era	fine–knife	star–rats

Variation

Apart from 'mirror words' like those in Box 40, there are other ways of pairing words, e.g.:

- on the basis of initial consonant clusters: *scratch, scramble, scraggy,* etc.; *groan, grumble, green,* etc.; *stretch, strain, strong,* etc.
- on the basis of words which can combine with a given stem word: *time-limit, time-lapse, time-bomb, time-capsule*; or conversely: *full-time, half-time, part-time, overtime, prime-time, closing time, quality time,* etc.
- on the basis of rhyme: *low, go, show, bow, mow, slow,* etc.

Note

In teaching vocabulary we often encourage learners to pair words in terms of synonymy or antonymy. This activity is a different way of finding relationships between words. It helps students to play with words – an important part of forming associations between words.

See also 4.11 A vocal tapestry, 8.7 Praise songs.

8.11 Charades

Aim	To dramatise the meaning of words syllable by syllable
Focus	Expressions of speculation, clarification; vocabulary will depend on the specifics of words chosen
Level	Upper-Intermediate–Advanced
Time	One class hour
Preparation	Make a list of words which lend themselves to being acted out syllable by syllable. Write them on slips of paper. Here are some examples: *o/pen, peo/ple, ten/sion, term/in/at/or, a/gain, ex/press, psycho/path, terr/if/y/ing, in/side, under/stand, humor/ous, in/de/pend/ent, for/get, real/ise, deter/mine, pers/e/cut/ion, con/firm, para/lyse, tre/mend/ous, ant/i/cip/ation, in/stance, ten/nis, in/tell/igent, never/the/less.*

Procedure

1 You will need to explain, then demonstrate, how charades works. The idea is that an individual (or group) has a word that they convey to others by miming and using sounds (but not words). Usually this is done by breaking the word into chunks and acting out each chunk separately, e.g. if the word was *tennis*, you might show ten fingers, then point at your knees; if the word was *humorous,* you could start by laughing a lot, then point to yourself and others to show *us*; if the word was *detestation*, you could make a face showing hate/disgust, then mime waiting for a train at a station.

2 When students have the idea, divide them into groups of five. Give one word slip to one person in each group. This student then has to present the word as quickly as possible to the other group members.

3 As soon as groups correctly guess the first word, give out a different slip to another group member. Continue with the activity till everyone has had a turn.

4 Conduct whole-class feedback, inviting volunteers to present some of their words to everyone. What were the most ingenious mimes?

Follow-on

For homework, ask students to find at least three more words which could be used in charades. Collect these in and use them in a repeat of the activity in a later lesson.

Notes

1   Students rapidly get the hang of this game and show remarkable ingenuity in putting the words across.
2   Like 3.12 Hotel receptionist, the activity tends to reactivate a wide range of vocabulary from the student's memory store.

See also 3.12 Hotel receptionist.

8.12   Split headlines

Aim	To encourage interaction through content/syntactic matching
Focus	This will depend on the specifics of the headlines chosen
Level	Intermediate and above
Time	30 minutes approximately
Preparation	Cut out a number of newspaper headlines – enough for one between every two students. Cut the headlines in half at an appropriate point. Box 41 provides some examples.

Procedure

1   Distribute the half-headlines at random, so that everyone has one.
2   Students memorise what is on their slip of paper. They then put the slip of paper away and do not refer to it again until the end. Students circulate, speaking their mini-text to everyone they meet. They do this as expressively as they can. They are looking for a match to form a complete headline. If they find a possible match, they should not stop as there may be a better one somewhere.
3   When everyone has found at least one match, hold a class feedback session where students call out their headlines, as dramatically as possible, and you write them on the board.

Note

The focus is not on the language of newspaper headlines – but you might want to use this activity as a way in to the language of newspapers.

See also 8.13 Split exchanges.

Box 41   Elementary

MARADONNA'S	DRUG PROBLEM
HIGHER TAXES	ON CIGARETTES
PRINCESS ANNE'S DOG	BITES TOURIST
BOMB SCARE	AT LONDON STATION
BEATLES ARE	STILL TOP OF THE POPS
TOUGH NEW LAW	AGAINST ILLEGAL WORKERS
BIG STORMS	CAUSE FLOODS

More advanced

WHY PETROL PRICES	NEED NOT RISE
STAY IN BED AND	CALL THE POLICE
POLICE FACE CRACKDOWN	ON DATA
BATTERED MEN GET	THEIR OWN REFUGE
POLICE CALL FOR REMOTE BUTTON	TO STOP CARS
BRITAIN BRACED	FOR BIG GETAWAY
WHY ALCOHOL IS SO	DAMAGING FOR YOUNG WOMEN
WASHED OUT:	NOT WASHED UP
THE MONSTERS	WE MAKE
WORST CHRISTMAS	FOR YEARS
FISHING CHIEFS	CLINCH QUOTA DEAL
THERE IS A BALANCE	TO BE STRUCK
UNITED	FACE WORLDWIDE BAN
POET GOES TO COURT	TO CLEAR HIMSELF OF MURDER

8.13 Split exchanges

Aim	To develop interaction on the basis of conversational fragments
Focus	Listening comprehension to develop a sense of appropriate responses; vocabulary will be specific to the particular exchanges
Level	Lower–Intermediate and above
Time	30 minutes approximately
Preparation	Prepare a number of conversational one-line utterances and one or more possible follow-on lines for each of them. Each line should be on separate slips of paper. You need enough copies for one per student. Box 42 provides some examples.

Procedure

1   Explain that students will be given a slip of paper with a sentence on it. They should then try to find other students with sentences which match their own. Explain that there may be many possible 'fits' with other sentences. It is a question of creating new combinations rather than simply finding the 'right' ones. For example, *There's a parrot in the fridge* could be followed by any of the following utterances:

    Would you like me to wrap it up for you?
    Would you like me to take it out for you?
    I think it's immoral.

    as well as by the more obvious matches, such as, *A parrot? Impossible!*

2   Distribute one slip of paper per student. They should memorise what is on their slip and practise saying it till they feel confident.

3   Students mingle freely, saying their utterances to each other. Whenever they find a 'fit', they should write down the exchange in their notebook so as not to forget it. They then continue to mingle and try to find another 'fit'. Tell them the 'fit' may be amusing or dramatic; it does not have to be obviously conventional. Allow up to 15 minutes for this.

4   Hold a class feedback session in which anyone can start an exchange by speaking one of the lead-in utterances. Anyone who has a sentence which could match this then speaks it out. See how many exchanges can be generated by a single utterance. Ask students who contribute an utterance what they think the context might be. Who are the speakers? What is their relationship? What is the topic? Where are they? etc.

Follow-on

In a later class, ask students, working in groups of three, to choose one of the lead-in utterances and to develop a short dramatisation of the encounter.

Box 42

1 There's a parrot in the fridge.

A parrot? Impossible!

Who told you that?

That's a ridiculous thing to say.

----

2 Do you know what myxomatosis is?

Something to do with rabbits, I think.

I haven't the faintest idea.

Are you kidding me?

----

3 I'm sorry, sir, but you can't go in there.

Do you realise who I am?

I'll do what I like!

Why don't you just mind your own business for a change?

----

4 Would you like me to wrap it up for you?

Don't worry. I'll take it as it is.

If you don't mind, yes.

----

5 I've got a splinter in my toe.

Would you like me to take it out for you?

Whose fault is that?

----

6 O that this too solid flesh would melt!

Box 42 *continued*

You can say that again.

Are you on a diet or something?

7 Have you ever been convicted of a serious offence?

Well, it all depends on what you mean …

Why do you ask me that?

8 Have you ever had malaria?

No. Why do you ask?

As a matter of fact, I have.

9 Didn't I see you with Sandra last night?

You'd better keep your mouth shut about that.

10 We're going to Las Vegas for a holiday.

You're throwing your money away.

Some people have all the luck.

11 She's just won first prize in the National Lottery.

I think it's immoral.

It won't make her any happier.

Note

This is a very productive and funny activity. It is, however, important that students understand that any utterance may match more than one other, and that they should look for creative combinations.

See also 8.12 Split headlines.

8.14 People, places, problems and things

Aim	To use random inputs to develop a dramatised scenario
Focus	Vocabulary can be partly controlled by the inputs but not wholly predicted; the main focus will be on the language of discussion, used to arrive at the end-product
Level	Intermediate and above
Time	One class hour
Preparation	You need to prepare cards or slips of paper with sentences or phrases relating to 'theme catchphrases' and 'scenes'. You need enough for one copy of each per group of five students. Box 43 provides some examples.

Procedure

1   Students work in groups of five. Give each group one Theme catchphrase and one Scene card at random. Allow ten minutes for groups to discuss their two cards and how they might link them together in a story.

2   Give groups 20 minutes to work out their dramatised story in detail. They need to decide who the characters are, what happens, what the dialogue will be, how the scene relates to the catchphrase, etc.

3   Each group performs its dramatised story for another group, followed by discussion and comment.

Note

Once again, as in other activities, it is the very lack of detailed inputs which stimulates students to find interesting and creative story lines.

See also 6.10 Faces and places.

Box 43

Theme catchphrases

Crime doesn't pay.	Live now, pay later.	Nobody loves me.	It's not fair!

Men (or women) are all the same.	You'll regret it later.	I couldn't care less.	It could be worse.

Scenes

At a supermarket	At the Taj Mahal	In an airport	On a building site

In the middle of the desert	On a riverboat in Bangkok	On a crowded country bus in India	In the British Museum

8.15 Odd news

Aim	To use fragments of news to generate coherent story lines
Focus	This will depend on the fragments chosen; language of discussion
Level	Intermediate and above
Time	One class hour
Preparation	Collect fragments from radio or TV broadcasts in English or from English-language newspapers. The fragments should be taken from a variety of sources, and not be longer than about ten words. Box 44 provides some examples. You will need a minimum of six fragments for each group of five students.

Procedure

1   Students work in groups of five. Distribute six or seven fragments to each group (each group gets the same fragments).

2   Allow 20 minutes for groups to find a way of linking the fragments into a connected story. One student, acting as group secretary, should write out the story. Group members then practise reading it 'dramatically' – either individually or as a group.

3   Each group performs its story for the rest of the class. Follow this by whole-class discussion and feedback. How different were the stories? How well were they performed? etc.

Follow-on
The stories can be displayed on the class noticeboard, along with the fragments.

Variations
1   Give each group a different set of fragments. Groups then exchange their stories with each other.

2   As a preparation for this activity, ask students, for homework, to collect five fragments each. These could be drawn from newspapers, radio/TV or (in the case of students living in an English-speaking country) from fragments of conversations they may have overheard in restaurants, shops or on public transport. For lower-level students, limit the number of words to five, e.g. *Have some tea.* Higher-level students can cope with longer fragments.

Box 44

Simpler

… but that was when I was young, of course.

… and I don't think he knew about it.

… before that I was in the army.

Who knows whether she really loved him. I certainly don't.

He had long hair and a long grey beard at the time.

Did she ever mention the war to you?

How did it feel to meet a monster like that?

Do you ever worry about the dangers involved?

More demanding

… produce about 60% of the bread eaten in England.

… and suddenly they have a pet – a cat, a horse, a dog, a donkey …

… bananas or oranges. They didn't even know how to peel an orange …

… What happens in this story? Well, there's this magpie …

… fishing rights, oil prices and the problem of …

… and how many times have we heard that argument before?

… but will she be able to get the world to vote for her?

8.16 Proverbs in action

Aim To use well-known English proverbs as the basis for dramatic interpretations

Focus Expressions of speculation; questions for clarification; vocabulary will be specific to the proverbs chosen

Level Upper-intermediate–Advanced

Time One class hour

Preparation Make a list of common English proverbs. Put them on the board or on an OHP transparency. You will also need to prepare slips of paper/cards bearing one proverb each. Box 45 provides some examples.

Procedure

1 You will need to explain at least some of the proverbs, since proverbs are often highly condensed, and sometimes the meaning may not be immediately clear, e.g. *He who hesitates is lost* is fairly clear, but *It's a long road …* is not immediately clear (it means that however long we have to wait, something good will happen eventually).

2 Students work in pairs. Each pair is given one proverb to work with. Allow 15 minutes for pairs to discuss their proverb and to rehearse a short dramatisation to show the meaning of it.

3 Each pair performs its dramatisation for the whole class. The class has to work out which of the proverbs listed on the board (or OHP) is being presented.

Follow-on

For homework, ask students to find some proverbs from their own language which are approximately equivalent to the English ones they worked with in the activity. In a later class, use these as the basis for a discussion of proverbs: where they come from, why they survive, why they seem to be repeated in all cultures, etc.

Note

It can be argued that proverbs are not so important in everyday communication. Like idioms, they have to be used with care. However, they do offer a stimulating starting point, both for drama work and for cross-cultural comparison and discussion.

Box 45

Time and tide wait for no man.	There's many a slip between cup and lip.	Don't put all your eggs in one basket.	A stitch in time saves nine.
Look before you leap.	He who hesitates is lost.	Many hands make light work.	Too many cooks spoil the broth.
The proof of the pudding is in the eating.	Distance lends enchantment to the view.	Every cloud has a silver lining.	It's a long road that has no turning.
Take care of the pence and the pounds will take care of themselves.	A rolling stone gathers no moss.	It's no good crying over spilt milk.	There's no fool like an old fool.
Beggars can't be choosers.	Least said, soonest mended.	Faint heart never won fair lady.	He who laughs last, laughs longest.

8.17 First lines

Aim	To encourage creative and dramatic manipulation of the first lines of poems
Focus	Syntactic recombination; speaking in a variety of styles
Level	Advanced
Time	One class hour
Preparation	Make a list of first lines from poems in English. Prepare cards with about six of these lines. Each card should be different. You will need one card per group of four. Box 46 provides some examples.

Procedure

1 Students work in groups of four. Give one card with first lines to each group.

2 Groups discuss the lines on the card for meaning. If the lines are incomplete, they suggest ways of completing them. Each student then takes one line only and decides how to read it for maximum expressive effect. Students read their lines to each other within the group. Allow ten minutes for this.

3 Write the following on the board or on an OHP transparency:
   • like a small child complaining to its mother
   • like a very old person remembering their past
   • like a TV chat show host
   • like a politician making an election speech.
   Tell students that they should practise speaking their sentences 'in role' as each of the four people listed on the board. Allow ten minutes for them to do this for the others in their group.

4 In a class feedback session, ask some students to perform their lines 'in role' for the whole class, without saying which role they are playing. The class has to guess the role. Can students suggest other roles/ways of speaking their lines?

5 Back in groups, students try to find a way of combining at least five of their sentences into a short dramatic scene. They rehearse this. They can be asked to perform their dramatisations in the next class.

Follow-on

If students enjoyed this activity, set a homework task in which each student finds five first lines on a given theme, e.g. city life, travel, nature, love, war, etc. In a later class, use these lines for a repeat of the activity.

Box 46

I am a man now
As I lay asleep in Italy
Because I liked you better
From my father, my strong heart
The sea is calm tonight
I have lived in important places, times

Move him into the sun
Nobody heard him, the dead man
This is the end of him, here he lies
I was angry with my friend
Let us go then, you and I
Everyone suddenly burst out singing

You did not walk with me
What is it to grow old
Your Beauty, ripe, and calm, and fresh
You stood with your back to me
Woman much missed, how you call to me, call to me
I have been young, and now am not too old

A city plum is not a plum
A picture has no grammar
The high hills have a bitterness
I have been here before
Even in the bluest noonday of July
The mountain sheep are sweeter

Note

The combination of first lines to make a new text is not a new idea, but it can be very suggestive of new meanings. It can also be very funny: see Tom Stoppard's abbreviated versions of *Hamlet* (1976) and *Macbeth* (1979), for instance, in which he chooses a few lines from the play and puts them together to make a very short new play.

Some resources for the activities in this chapter

For names:

Dunkling, L. (1986) *The Guiness Book of Names*, Guiness Publishing.

Dunkling, L. and Gosling, W. (1991) *The New American Dictionary of Baby Names*, New American Library.

Dunkling, L. and Wright, G. (1994) *Pub Names of Britain*, Orion.

For proverbs:

Brewer's Dictionary of Phrase and Fable (1975), Revised by Ivor Evans, Cassell.

Wilson, F. P. (ed) (1970) *The Oxford Dictionary of English Proverbs*, Oxford: OUP.

For word games:

Augarde, T. (1996) *The Oxford A to Z of Word Games*, Oxford: OUP.

Crystal, D. (1998) *Language Play*, London: Penguin.

Espey, W.R. (1971) *The Game of Words*, London: Wolfe Pubs.

9 Working from/into texts

In this chapter, we shall be using texts as a way into dramatisation. It is important to distinguish between texts (prose or poetry) and scripts of plays or sketches, which we shall deal with in Chapter 10. Scripts come ready-made, even if we need to interpret them in individual ways. By contrast, texts are not initially designed for dramatisation, yet they contain within them the seeds of dramatic action. They can therefore be made the starting point for characterisation, for a narrative plot or for a scene involving dramatic tension, including dialogue. Such texts bring alive visualisations in our minds; they begin to paint pictures in our heads, to awaken dialogue, to suggest a wider context. As we read even a banal newspaper article, we begin to form our own personal impression of the incident described; and it is probably true to say that, the shorter and less specific the text, the more productive it may be – inviting us to supply more of the detail for ourselves. Such texts evoke, they do not define.

9.1 Mini-texts

Aim	To invent a story line and dramatisation from a mini-text
Focus	Vocabulary will depend on the text chosen; language of discussion and evaluation; dialogue
Level	Intermediate and above
Time	One class hour
Preparation	You will need a number of very short, evocative texts, which do not have much detail. Box 47 provides some examples.

Procedure

1 Divide the class into three groups (or any multiple of three: six, nine, etc.) and give each group a different text, e.g. if you are working with the texts in set 2, give d) to group A, e) to group B and f) to group C. Allow groups ten minutes to read and discuss their texts. Who is speaking? Where are they? What are the relationships? What is the situation in detail?

2 Now allow students 20 minutes to create a dialogue, involving at least two people. They can use some of the language from the text but they will also need to generate some of their own. They will also need to create at

least one new character who does not figure in the original text. Their dialogues should reflect the interpretation they arrived at in step 1.

3 Each group nominates one member to read the original text in an expressive, dramatic way. Another group member will outline the group's interpretation. Two other group members will then perform the dialogue for the rest of the class (if there are six or nine groups, each text will be performed more than once, allowing for comparisons to be made).

Follow-on

1 In a later class, groups look at all three texts and dialogues (you will need to prepare these in advance). Is there a way of linking these three texts/dialogues into a complete short play?

2 The original texts and the dialogues they evoked can be made into a wall display.

Note

The texts offer no more than hints about the total situation thus stimulating many different possible interpretations. Much of the value of this (and other activities in this section) lies in the discussion process as much as the final dialogue product.

See also 6.16 Characters from fiction.

Box 47

Set 1

a) I am here. You are there. Here and there. You and I. A long way apart.

----

b) I know I can't get it. It's impossible. It's useless even to try. I know. But the trouble is, I can't live without it.

----

c) I went. I spoke to them. They were polite and cold. They didn't understand. They promised to try again.

Set 2

d) You came. You were late. As usual. But you came. It was a rainy day. But you came. And sunshine filled the world. And music filled the world. Though it was raining. And grey.

----

e) You said you'd come in your car to collect me. 'At nine o'clock,' you said. In front of my house. It's nearly nine. Dressed up I look at the gate. I wait. Between nine and ten. Every day. Why don't you come?

----

f) It's six. She should be here any moment now. Quarter past. Late as usual. Half past. She must come. Will she? What if she doesn't? Telephone? Yes … No answer. She must have left. Must be on the way. What if she isn't?

Set 3

g) He never sent me flowers. He never wrote me letters. He never took me to restaurants. He never spoke of love. We met in parks. I don't remember what he said, but I remember how he said it. Most of it was silence anyway.

----

h) Enough. I've had enough. Don't explain anything. I don't want to hear. I've heard it all before. Don't be ridiculous. I can't stand it. You are wasting your time. Yes, I've made up my mind. And I'm not going to change it.

----

i) You know the facts. Why? Why did I do it? It's difficult to explain. I wouldn't like to lie. I know you have the right to know. But I can't tell you. Not because I don't want to. I know it would be better if I did. Better for all of us. But I can't. I simply can't. And you can't help me. So don't try to.

LESZEK SZKUTNIK *Thinking in English*

9.2 What next?

Aim	To use a short text to stimulate a dramatic dialogue
Focus	Vocabulary will depend on choice of text; language of spoken interaction
Level	Intermediate–Advanced
Time	One class hour
Preparation	You need a number of short texts which set a scene without specifying what people say to each other. Box 48 provides some examples.

Procedure

1 Explain that students will be working on a text which has little or no dialogue in it, but which sets up a situation or problem in which language is needed. Give an example, if necessary:

The Mother

Of course I love them, they are my children.
That is my daughter and this is my son.
And this is my life I give them to please them.
It has never been used. Keep it safe. Pass it on.

ANNE STEVENSON

Who is speaking? To whom? (A marriage counsellor? An old friend? Her husband? etc.) What might they then talk about? Collect ideas from the class about what they might say.

2 Students work in groups of five. Distribute two copies of the text you have chosen to each group. Allow 20 minutes for them to interpret the text and to brainstorm some of the things the speakers might say to each other.

3 Collect these ideas in whole-class feedback. Allow groups another 15 minutes to write out the dialogue they have agreed upon. Groups then perform their mini-drama for the rest of the class.

Follow-on

1 Students prepare a wall display of the dialogue texts they have derived from the original text.

2 If the activity really catches fire, it can be developed into a full-scale class dramatisation, all based on the seed of the original text.

Note

The function of the original text is to act as a catalyst for interpretation of the issue (in the examples in Box 49: the pain of a relationship, the anger between lovers, the trust/mistrust between married couples, etc.) and then to map words on to the situation as interpreted.

Box 48

They sat facing each other across the table in the coffee bar. He was older than her. She did not speak. Neither did he. He looked at her all the time but she kept her eyes down. He reached across to touch her hand. She pulled it away violently. Then she began to cry – silently. The tears ran down her cheeks but she made no attempt to wipe them away.

ALAN MALEY

The Lovers

After the tiff there was stiff silence, till
One word, flung in centre like single stone,
Starred and cracked the ice of her resentment
To its edge. From that stung core opened and
Poured up one outward and widening wave
Of eager and extravagant anger.

W. R. ROGERS

The Inner Man

Their marriage was
a perfect union of trust
and understanding. They
shared everything – except
his desk drawer, which,
through the years remained
locked.
One day, curiosity
overcame her. Prised open,
there was – nothing.
'But why,' she asked,
confused and ashamed.
'I needed a space of my
own,' he replied sadly.

CHRISTINE M. BANKS

The President and Vice-President were out campaigning. They stopped for lunch. The attractive young waitress asked, 'What will you have?'
'I think I'll have a quickie,' said the President. She slapped his face. 'You may be President but …'
The Vice-President leant across the table. 'I think it's pronounced *quiche*,' he said.

© CAMBRIDGE UNIVERSITY PRESS 2005

9.3 Starters

Aim	To use the openings of stories as starters for developing a story line and dramatisation
Focus	Vocabulary will depend on the extracts chosen; language of discussion and evaluation; spoken dialogue
Level	Intermediate and above
Time	One class hour
Preparation	You need enough copies of the opening of a short story, one for every two students. Box 49 provides some examples.

Procedure

1 Working with the whole class, take the first line of a short story, e.g.:
   Since he returned from the war things had not been quite the same.
   ARUN JOSHI *The Homecoming*
   Ask students to suggest what the next sentence might be. Then the next, and so on. How does this story develop?
2 Students work in groups of four. You give two copies of the story opening to each group. Allow 20 minutes for them to develop a story line from the text. Their stories should involve at least three characters. Remind them that a story has to have a plot – something has to happen.
3 Check on students' stories in a whole-class feedback session.
4 Allow another 15 minutes for students to dramatise their stories with dialogue and movement.
5 Finally, groups perform their stories for the rest of the class.

Follow-on
You could give out the complete original story for students to read as homework, so that they can compare it with their own versions.

Variation
Distribute different first lines to each group. Each group works out its story line based on this first line. They then exchange their story lines with another group. They prepare the dramatised version on the basis of the story line they have received (not their own original one).

Note
For a writer, the first few lines of a story are the most difficult to write, for they determine how it will develop. In this case, the beginning is determined but students can use their own imagination to decide how it will continue.

See also 9.1 Mini-texts.

Box 49

Intermediate

Miriam sat at the window, looking down at the street. It was Friday evening. People were already leaving their offices and the shops were closing. Soon she would be alone again – as usual.   ALAN MALEY *It was Friday evening …*

Bram sat in the corner of his cell, facing the wall. (Actually, it was a comfortably-furnished room, with all the latest conveniences.) For days he had been resisting the constant battery of commercials which the screens on every wall pumped out at him.   ALAN MALEY *Death on Credit*

The fields stretched away flat to the horizon. It was dawn. Ben stood at the bedroom window, Karen's cup of tea in his hand. He wondered if he should mention the smoke to her.   ALAN MALEY *No Smoking*

It was evening in the private room at the hospital. I moved to put on the light. 'No. Not yet. I can't talk to you with the light on.'
          ALAN MALEY *Words Long Unspoken*

Advanced

A message came from the rescue party, who straightened up and leaned on their spades in the rubble. The policeman said to the crowd, 'Everyone keep quiet for five minutes. No talking, please. They're trying to hear where he is.'
          V. S. PRITCHETT *The Voice*

I smile as I hear them at last, the sounds I am waiting for. A rush of footsteps, the slam of a bathroom door … I wince as the sound whams through the silent house … and, a minute later, another bang. And then, bare feet running towards me.
          SHASHI DESHPANDE *My Beloved Charioteer*

'The marvellous thing is that it's painless,' he said, 'That's how you know when it starts.'
'Is it really?'
'Absolutely. I'm awfully sorry about the odour though. That must bother you.'

'Don't. Please, don't.'
'Look at them,' he said. 'Now is it sight or is it scent that brings them like that?'
          ERNEST HEMINGWAY *The Snows of Kilimanjaro.*

195

Box 49 *continued*

Eight o'clock in the morning. Miss Ada Moss lay in a black iron bedstead, staring up at the ceiling. Her room, a Bloomsbury top-floor back, smelled of soot and face powder and the paper of fried potatoes she brought in for supper the night before. 'Oh dear,' thought Miss Moss, 'I am cold. I wonder why it is that I always wake up cold in the mornings now …'

KATHERINE MANSFIELD *Pictures*

© CAMBRIDGE UNIVERSITY PRESS 2005

9.4 Tops and tails

Aim	To use a text as a springboard for prediction and dramatisation
Focus	Vocabulary will depend on the specific texts chosen; language of discussion and evaluation; spoken dialogue
Level	Intermediate and above
Time	One class hour
Preparation	You will need a number of short texts which are in some way enigmatic, i.e. it is not absolutely clear what the topic is. Box 50 provides some examples.

Procedure

1 Distribute one text per group of three students. Allow ten minutes for them to discuss it. Who is speaking? Where are they? Who are they speaking to? What are they speaking about? Students try to 'situate' the text as fully as possible.

2 Groups feed back their ideas in a whole-class session.

3 Back in groups, students try to add some text at the beginning (the top) and at the end (the tail) of the fragment they are working with. The text they add should make it clear what the situation is. It may be spoken by the same person or by others. Allow 20 minutes for this.

4 Allow groups ten minutes to prepare to perform their texts. Each group then performs for the whole class.

Box 50

Lower-Intermediate

a) Why did she agree? That was very stupid. Now what?

b) There's no hope. I'm very sorry. I really didn't expect this. What can I say?

c) It was just wonderful. I wish you could have seen her. I'll never forget it. Never.

d) How much longer? I can't stand this waiting. Can't you do anything?

Intermediate

a) This makes everything possible. I wonder if she realises that? Now she'll be the centre of attention. Everyone will want her. I just hope she doesn't …

b) I told you before: it's too late. You can't stop it now. You did it, and you can't undo it. Now we just have to try to …

c) No one knows how long it would take. We've looked at the figures. We've worked out how many people we need. But there are things we just don't know. How often do they change the serial numbers, for instance?

d) But that's how it is. We can't change things. It's a bit like a flower. You plant the seeds in spring. You watch it grow. The bud forms and opens into a lovely bloom. Then the petals fall off. It dries up, and dies. Then we think, never mind, it will grow again next year. But, of course, people are not the same as flowers, are they?

Advanced

a) Figures are not everything. What does a hundred mean, or a thousand? Nor is size as important as we think. What is big? What is small? Everything is relative. What is important, then? Time? Space? Freedom of movement? Perhaps. But surely, what matters most is knowing that the fire is still burning, and that the lights have not gone out.

b) Black. Green. Yellow. Red. These are not just colours. They are more than colours. Each has a quality of its own. A different quality. How can we discover this if we do not search? But you can search and not find. There are those for whom green and red, yellow and black are still no more than colours. They are the ones who have searched and not found.

c) I don't know why we weren't made like that. We could have been given special guns, which we could deter people with, but as soon as we used them they'd fire in both directions, backwards and forwards, so you'd shoot yourself at the same time. That would put an end to all this violence in the streets.[1]

[1] From Peter Cook (2003) 'A Bee Life', in *Tragically I was an Only Twin: the Complete Peter Cook*, Arrow Books, p. 73.

Follow-on

1   If there is time, prepare a display of all the versions of the completed text.
2   You may wish to use the texts produced by groups as input for discourse analysis. Some will have a better 'fit' than others. Why is this? Which textual features make a text more cohesive and coherent?

Variations

1   Give a different text to each group. Then omit step 2 but spend longer on the discussion of each performance in step 4.
2   Take a text which can be split into several fragments. Give each group a different fragment. They proceed as above (omitting step 2). When they reach the final stage, distribute the original complete text so that they can compare their 'tops and tails' with what the text actually contained. One possible source for such monologues is Alan Bennett (1988) *Talking Heads*, BBC Books.

Notes

1   This activity provides plenty of opportunities for contextualisation, and for the exercise of visualisation and imaginative projection.
2   The activity also helps students develop an eye and an ear for the tone and style of the text.

See also 9.1 Mini-texts, 9.3 Starters.

9.5 Jumbled stories

Aim	To develop a dramatised version of a short narrative text
Focus	Vocabulary will depend on the content of the story; language of discussion; transfer from written to spoken language
Level	Intermediate and above
Time	One class hour
Preparation	You will need the text of a relatively short story with a clear point. (Urban Myths are a good source. See also *Short!: a book of very short stories* by Kevin Crossley-Holland [1998], OUP.) The text should be cut up (as in the example in Box 51), divided into ten sections.

Procedure

1 Explain that each group of ten students will be given ten fragments of a story. (If it is more convenient, groups of five can be formed – each student receiving two fragments.) They have to reconstruct the story by sharing their fragments orally (they are not allowed to show their slips to anyone). Allow 15 minutes for this.

2 Check with the whole class that the story has been reconstructed by all groups, and has been understood.

3 Groups develop a dramatisation of the incident in the story. This will involve movement, dialogue (and perhaps a commentator). Allow 20 minutes for this. Groups then perform their pieces for the whole class, followed by evaluation and discussion.

Box 51

An English couple and their two teenage children were touring Australia.

They wanted to see the 'real outback' with its desert landscapes and its wildlife.

They hired a car and drove off into the outback.

On the second day, as they were driving along, miles from anywhere, a kangaroo hopped out into the road in front of them.

The man tried to stop but he couldn't. He hit the kangaroo, which bounced off the car, and lay motionless by the road.

Thinking it was dead, the man had an idea. He took off his jacket and put it on the kangaroo. Then he put his sunglasses on it.

His wife and kids stood behind the kangaroo, which they held up to face the camera.

As the man took the picture, the kangaroo suddenly jumped up and ran away across the desert, wearing the man's jacket and sunglasses.

In the pocket of his jacket were the car keys, the man's credit card, his wallet with all his money, and his passport.

An expensive photograph!

© CAMBRIDGE UNIVERSITY PRESS 2005

Follow-on
On the display board, groups can put up a typed version of their 'drama' alongside the written version in Box 51.

Note
The activity moves from comprehension via discussion and reconstruction, to expression, since students have to transfer their understanding of narrative to the creation of a direct representation of it.

9.6 What are they saying?

Aim	To develop a playscript from a fiction extract
Focus	Vocabulary will depend on the texts chosen; spoken language derived from written (direct from indirect or reported speech)
Level	Intermediate–Advanced
Time	At least one class hour
Preparation	You need to find an extract from a novel or short story which has potential for dialogue, and which can be broken up into a number of fragments. Box 52 provides some examples.

Procedure

1 Divide the class into multiples of three (if you use stories with three episodes). Explain that each group will have a part of the text, and that they will have to rewrite their fragment as dialogue plus stage directions. You may need to show how this is to be done:

> Lakshmi accompanies him to the street. They stand by his car for a moment.
> Dick: *It was lovely to meet you.*
> Lakshmi: *It was for me too. When …* (she hesitates)
> Dick: *Sorry?*
> Lakshmi: *Oh, nothing.*
> Dick: *Lakshmi, when can we meet again?*
> Lakshmi: *Oh, Dick. I don't know. It's my father …*

2 Give out a different extract to each group. Allow up to 30 minutes for them to read and discuss it, and to write out their part of the playscript.

3 Each group performs its dialogue dramatisation for the rest of the class, in order from a) to c). If more than one group has the same extract, all the a) extracts perform together, then all the b) extracts, etc.

Box 52

Example 1

a) The police report said that he met her outside the station. They spoke for a few minutes. Then they got into a taxi.

b) The taxi driver told us that the couple talked a lot, in whispers. She was showing him a letter. They seemed very tense.

c) In the café, the man and woman got into an argument. She kept waving a letter at him. He seemed very angry. Suddenly she got up, spilling her coffee over him, and ran out of the café.

Example 2

a) The three men were sitting by a lake. They were fishing. They were boasting about all the big fish they had caught in the past.

b) Suddenly, one man's line goes tight. He is very excited, and pulls in – an old boot. The others laugh. Then the second man pulls in – an old bicycle wheel. They all laugh at him too. Then the third man pulls in – a dead dog! They decide not to tell anyone at the pub about their catch of the day!

c) In the pub, the three men are boasting about the size of the fish they caught today. (Of course, they threw these enormous fish back into the lake!) No one believes them.

Example 3

a) While Lakshmi busied herself preparing lunch, Nagarajan told Dick that she was a widow. He had arranged her marriage to a boy from the same community, a computer software specialist. They had married at the boy's home town, near Udipi, when she was twenty-two. By then she had completed her MA in English literature. It was time for babies, grandchildren to warm old people's hearts, and to justify their years of work and struggle. But no children came. And, five years later Girijan, her husband, had died in a motorcycle accident.

Box 52 *continued*

b) Nagarajan's confused conversation was interrupted when Lakshmi brought them lunch. It was simple vegetarian food – rice, dal and vegetable masala with chappaties – but the aroma was delicious. Lakshmi, in traditional Indian style, did not eat with them – she would eat later.

c) It was some time before Lakshmi returned to clear the dishes. She said nothing and went about her work with her eyes lowered, not looking at Dick. As she was about to leave the room, Dick asked her, 'How is your father? What has happened to him?'

d) Dick left her father slumped in an old armchair in the corner of the darkening room, still smoking. The sound of his coughing followed Dick out. Lakshmi accompanied him to the street. His car was waiting. They stood for a moment before he got in.

ALAN MALEY *He Knows Too Much*

© CAMBRIDGE UNIVERSITY PRESS 2005

Follow on
1   In a later class, you might have groups performing the whole sequence as a complete play. They could add a concluding scene.
2   The way that speech is rendered in writing is far more complex than most of the simplified grammar books we use would have us think. If it is appropriate, you could analyse the way speech is dealt with in these texts.

Note
The dialogue can sometimes be retrieved from the text. Sometimes, however, dialogue can be added where it contributes to a better flow of the conversation.

9.7 Stop press

Aim	To develop dramatisation from short newspaper articles
Focus	Vocabulary will depend on articles chosen; language of discussion and evaluation; spoken dialogue
Level	Intermediate and above
Time	Two class hours
Preparation	You need to find a short newspaper article about an incident involving several people, which can form the basis of a dramatisation. Box 53 provides an example. Make three copies for each group of six.

Procedure

First class hour

1   Explain to students that they will be developing a short play from an incident described in a newspaper article. When they get the article, they should answer the following questions for themselves, making notes as they do so:
    • Who are the people involved? Make a list.
    • Where does this incident take place?
    • When did it happen?
    • What exactly happened (and how)? List the events in order of occurrence.
    • What were the consequences of this incident?
2   Give out copies of the article to each group of six (one copy between two). Allow 15 minutes for the questions in step 1. Then conduct whole-class feedback to make sure everyone has understood the article.
3   Groups work out a scenario based on the facts they have noted. They should decide how many scenes they will have, who will be in each scene, and what will be said and done. They should include scenes even if they are not explicitly described in the article, e.g. the scene between father and son when they first discover they are cut off by the tide; the scene after they have been rescued, etc. Allow 20 minutes for this. Then conduct class discussion comparing different groups' ideas.

Second class hour

4   Groups prepare dialogue for each of their scenes. Each group then performs its play for the whole class.

Note

This is quite a demanding activity and does need two lessons to complete if it is to be done properly. The stages are important: first, clearly understanding the incident in its full context; then, mapping out the scenes which will be needed to enact it; finally, putting words in the mouths of the characters.

Box 53

LIFEBOAT CREW RESCUES PAIR FROM ICY RIVER

Father and son were 'minutes from death'

Lifeboatmen faced a race against time to rescue a father and son cut off by a freak tide while out winter fowling.

By Ian Read

Joe Cranston, of Homewood Road, Sturry, was out with his 11-year-old son Aaron on the remote Slayhills Marsh on the River Medway, near Upchurch on Sunday morning.

He sparked a major air sea rescue operation by dialling 999 on his mobile phone and contacting coastguards who launched Sheerness Inshore Lifeboat.

At the same time an RAF Sea King helicopter was scrambled from RAF Wattisham in Suffolk.

The lifeboatmen found Mr Cranston up to his waist in cold water with the young lad sitting on his shoulders and their two dogs swimming in the water.

The high wind combined with the cold weather produced a sub-zero chill factor, lifeboatmen said.

Robin Castle, Coxswain of Sheerness Lifeboat said the high-speed rescue craft reached the stranded pair within half an hour of being called.

He said, 'The man and his son were out wild fowling when they were caught out by a higher-than-usual tide. 'Mr Cranston was up to his waist in water with the boy on his shoulders. They were cold but none the worse for their ordeal, and the inshore lifeboat was able to pick them up and deliver them to where their car was parked.

'Mr Cranston was able to ring Dover Coastguard who relayed his call to the operations centre at Clacton who called us out.

'The unusually high tide and the cold wind meant they could have drowned or been frozen if they had delayed calling for even a few more minutes. It was a life or death race, and because we were quick off the mark, we won.'

Neither Mr Cranston or Aaron needed medical attention but coastguards said they had a lucky escape.

Canterbury Christmas Special w/e 26 Dec, 2003

10 Working from/into scenarios and scripts

In this chapter, we come one step closer to actual performance. Scenarios are outlines of a dramatic situation, on to which the players then map words and actions. These are suggested by the scenario but not determined by it, so there is considerable scope for improvisation. Scripts, by contrast, actually specify the words to be spoken, and give a more or less detailed description of the characters and how they will move and speak. The players must still clothe the words with their own interpretations but they are circumscribed by the script, which is not normally changeable.

Both scenarios and scripts offer opportunities for students to put to use many of the skills they have acquired earlier in this book. In fact, before launching into a script, it will always be beneficial to do some warming-up exercises, for the body, the voice, and for general mental alertness. Just as an orchestra needs to tune up before playing, so do players of a script.

10.1 One-word dialogues

Aim	To practise a range of intonations in order to make explicit the meaning of minimal dialogue
Focus	Intonation; expansion of single-word into multi-word utterances
Level	Elementary and above
Time	One class hour
Preparation	You need to prepare a set of minimal dialogues, enough for one between every two students. Box 54 provides some examples.

Procedure

1 Distribute one copy of a dialogue to each pair of students. Allow ten minutes for them to decide who is talking, where they are and what they are talking about.
2 Check on students' ideas in a whole-class session.
3 Allow another ten minutes for students to rehearse speaking the dialogue. Each student should try both halves of the dialogue.
4 Pairs perform their dialogues in a whole-class session. This is when improvements, especially in the intonation, can be suggested.

5 Pairs spend another ten minutes expanding their dialogues to make the
meanings more explicit, e.g.

    A: *She's gone. She's left. She's not in her room.*
    B: *Really? Are you sure?*
    A: *This isn't the first time. She's done it before. Now she's run off
      again.*
    B: *Are you really surprised, after the way you treated her?*

Collect the students' scripts for correction and feedback in the next class.

Variation

Ask students to make up their own one-word dialogues. They exchange these
with a partner, who reads one part (A or B) and has to find an interpretation.

Note

Intonation is notoriously tricky to teach in English, partly because linguists
offer different and often conflicting descriptions, and partly because
intonation performs a multiplicity of functions. This activity allows students
to focus on minimal units of intonation to convey emphasis, querying,
appreciation, etc. This does not solve the problem but it helps, by limiting it.

See also 4.10 Working on words, 4.12 Shifting the stress, Chapter 11,
Improvisation and *Rehearsal*.

Box 54

A: Good.	A: Late!
B: Good?	B: Late?
A: Good.	A: Yes!
B: OK. Well …	B: Sorry …
A: Speak up.	A: Gone.
B: Hush!	B: Really?
A: Why?	A: Again.
B: Because …	B: Surprised?

© CAMBRIDGE UNIVERSITY PRESS 2005

10.2 Dialogue interpretation

Aim	To encourage the imaginative interpretation of a script
Focus	Vocabulary will depend on the situations chosen; intonation to convey emotional charge, surprise, etc.; language of discussion and evaluation
Level	Lower-Intermediate and above
Time	One class hour
Preparation	You will need a number of short dialogues open to various interpretations – enough copies for one between two. Box 55 provides some examples.

Procedure

1 Students work in pairs. Distribute the same dialogue per pair. Explain that they have to set their dialogue in a specific context. They will need to decide who is speaking, where they are, what the topic is, what exactly is going on. Allow ten minutes for this.

2 In a whole-class session, collect ideas from students arising from their discussion.

3 Allow another ten minutes for pairs to rehearse their dialogues. Partners should take turns at reading A and B so that they each get the feel for the speaker. Finally, they perform their dialogues for the whole class.

4 Either in class, if there is time, or as homework, students should extend the dialogues into a slightly longer script, by adding a couple of lines at the beginning and some concluding lines. Encourage them to add stage directions, to give A and B names, etc.

Variation

Instead of giving the same dialogue to each pair, give out different ones to each pair, matching the difficulty level with the students' proficiency.

Note

In this activity, the dialogue acts both as a mini-script and as a starting point for a scenario. Unlike many textbook dialogues, which are, if anything, over-explicit, these dialogues leave ample room for students to exercise their creative imagination.

See also 4.10 Working on words, 4.12 Shifting the stress, 4.15 Playing with the text, Chapter 11, *Improvisation* and *Rehearsal*.

Box 55

Lower-Intermediate

1 A: Can you see them?
   B: No, where are they?
   A: Look, over there, behind that tree.
   B: Wow! That's really interesting!

2 A: How long?
   B: I'm not sure …
   A: But I need to know.
   B: Come back later then.

3 A: Please tell me.
   B: What can I tell you?
   A: You know what I mean.
   B: How CAN I tell you that?

4 A: Who did this?
   B: I'm not sure.
   A: But you must know. You were here all the time.
   B: I'm sorry … I can't … It's a secret.

Intermediate

1 A: It's time.
   B: What do you mean?
   A: I think you know what I mean.
   B: Oh no. Not yet, surely. It can't be.
   A: Come on now.

2 A: Well, after that, what more could I say?
   B: Mm. I can see it must have been difficult for you.
   A: Difficult!

3 A: As much as that? But was it worth it?
   B: Well, you know him as well as I do. Once he's made up his mind …
   A: Let's just hope he doesn't live to regret it.

4 A: Will it be enough, do you think?
   B: When is it ever enough?
   A: Yes. I wonder if they'll ever be satisfied.

10.3 Alibi

Aim	To use a simple scenario to give practice in asking and answering questions
Focus	All types of question forms; expressing degrees of certainty; challenging and responding to challenges
Level	All
Time	One class hour
Preparation	You need to be ready with a brief description of a crime: what crime it was, who the victim was, roughly when it took place, where it took place. Box 56 provides some examples.

Procedure

1 Explain what an alibi is (a reason why someone could not possibly have committed a particular crime because they were somewhere else at the time).

2 Describe the crime which has been committed. Tell students that they are all possible suspects.

3 Students work in pairs. Each pair must come to agreement on their alibi. They need to think about where they were at the time, who and what they saw. They should think about this in detail and remember it because both of them were together when the crime was committed. Allow ten minutes for this preparation. Students are not allowed to write down their alibis.

4 Select just one pair. Send one of the two students out of the classroom. The rest of the students then question the remaining student about their alibi. They should ask questions of detail and make sure they remember the answers.

5 After five to ten minutes, invite the other member of the pair back into the classroom. Students now ask this student the same questions they asked the first one. They are trying to find inconsistencies between the answers given by the partners. If there are inconsistencies, the pair are sent into custody. If not, they are freed.

6 Choose another pair and repeat the process.

Variation

Choose two students as suspects. They go outside the room and plan their story for ten minutes. While they are out, the rest of the class prepares their questions. One of the suspects is called in for five minutes' questioning. Then the other suspect comes in to answer the same questions. The class tries to uncover inconsistencies between the two stories.

Box 56

- Last Friday at about 8 pm, an old lady was coming out of the supermarket when a young teenager snatched her handbag and ran off.
- Some time between midnight and 5 am on Sunday morning, a Jaguar car was stolen from outside a house in Finchley, London. The owner, the distinguished conductor, Sir Fred Bolti, was away in Liverpool for a concert but his wife was at home.
- The 10-year-old son of footballer Billy Everton was kidnapped outside his school at 3.30 pm yesterday afternoon. His kidnappers are demanding payment of $2 million as ransom.

Notes

1 This activity is good preparation for dealing with the unpredictable in drama situations. However well the pairs try to predict the questions they will be asked, there will always be surprises. This will mean they will always have to 'think on their feet', trying to give the answer they hope their partner will give (or has given).

2 Students usually quickly realise that they need to ask questions about things the 'alibists' will not have thought of, such as: *What was the weather like?*, *What clothes were you wearing?*, *Did you hear the clock striking?* etc.

10.4 Just a minute

Aim	To practise the skills of interrupting (and dealing with interruptions)
Focus	Expressions used to interrupt a speaker: *Excuse me, Wait a minute, What are you talking about?, What do you mean?*, etc.; expressions used to deal with interruptions: *I'll come to that in a minute, I'll take questions at the end, not now, Would you please wait a minute! Just let me finish what I am saying first. Will you give me a chance to finish what I'm saying!* etc.
Level	Intermediate and above
Time	Up to one class hour
Preparation	You will need two poems or shortish monologues roughly at the students' language level. Box 57 provides two examples.

Procedure

1 Conduct a whole-class session eliciting ways of interrupting and dealing with interruptions. Depending on the level of the class, you may decide to write some of these on the board.

2 Divide the class into two. Give Group A one text, and Group B the other. Individually, students then prepare to read their text aloud. Allow ten minutes for this.

3 Choose one student from Group A to read their text aloud to the class. Tell the rest of the students that they should interrupt the reading with questions, comments, objections, etc. The student reading must somehow deal with these interruptions.

4 After five minutes, ask a student from Group B to read their text. Follow the same procedure. Continue the process until several students have had a turn.

5 Conduct another class feedback session. What additional expressions were used? Write these up on the board. If students have access to English language TV, ask them to check on what people do in interviews. How do they interrupt each other and respond to interruptions?

Variation

Instead of a text, simply ask students to tell a personal anecdote or a well-known folk story, e.g. *Goldilocks and the Three Bears* or *Little Red Riding Hood*.

Notes

1 In larger classes, you may have to split the class into groups of eight, giving four students one text and four the other. The activity then takes place within each group with class feedback at the end.

2 Choosing the right moment to interrupt, deciding how to do it (politely or rudely!) and what to say is a useful conversational skill. It is also useful in drama work, where speed of response is often important.

See also 4.16 Listen to me!, Chapter 11, *Improvisation* and *Rehearsal*.

Box 57

Intermediate

To M.M

The first time
we met as strangers
We parted as friends.

The second time
we met as friends
We parted as lovers

The last time
we met as lovers
We parted as friends

We did not meet
again
We are now
not even friends

GERALD ENGLAND

Advanced

Life, you know, is rather like opening a tin of sardines. We are all of us looking for the key. And, I wonder, how many of you here tonight have wasted years of your lives looking behind the kitchen dressers of this life for that key. I know I have. Others think they've found the key, don't they? They roll back the lid of the sardine tin of life, they reveal the sardines, the riches of life therein, and they get them out, they enjoy them. But, you know, there's always a little bit in the corner you can't get out. I wonder – I wonder, is there a little bit in the corner of your life? I know there is in mine.

ALAN BENNETT *Take a Pew*

10.5 Telephone conversations

Aim	To promote anticipation in a partially improvised dialogue
Focus	Vocabulary will depend on the choice of topic; asking and answering questions; clarification
Level	Lower-Intermediate and above
Time	One class hour
Preparation	You need to prepare a fragment of *one* half of a telephone conversation only. You need enough copies for one between every two students. Box 58 provides three examples: - - - indicates what the other person says (which we cannot hear).

Procedure

1 Explain that students will have only one half of a telephone conversation, and that they have to work out what the other half might be. This involves imaginative interpretation. Demonstrate how this might work on a small fragment:

> - - -
>
> *Next Monday? Yes, I suppose I can ask for a day off work for it. But when did he die?*
>
> - - -
>
> *That was sudden, wasn't it?*
>
> - - -
>
> *Oh, I hadn't realised he'd been in hospital so long.*

2 Students work in pairs. Distribute one copy of the half conversation to each pair. Allow 15 minutes for them to work on it together. They have to reconstitute the missing part. This should be written down.

3 Check on the ideas students have come up with in a whole-class session. This will be the time to offer corrections or suggestions for improvements.

4 Back in pairs, allow students ten minutes to improve their first drafts and to practise performing their telephone conversations.

5 In a smallish class, each pair then performs its conversation. They do this sitting back-to-back. In a larger class, each pair joins another pair and they perform for each other in turn.

Follow-on

1 You may wish to spend part of a later lesson looking in detail at the possible utterances which could fill each gap. This is a useful activity for studying spoken discourse.

2   As a homework assignment, ask students to write a short telephone conversation, then to write out a version with one speaker's utterances removed (as in the examples). In a later lesson, students can exchange their gapped versions with a partner and try to supply the missing utterances.

Variation

You may prefer to work on a theatre script. Box 59 provides an example.

Box 58

Lower-Intermediate

\- - -

Wow! That's great! What was the score?

\- - -

I don't believe it!

\- - -

I'm sure they did. Was there any trouble?

\- - -

Thank goodness for that!

- -

Intermediate

\- - -

Did you? I didn't realise you knew her.

\- - -

In Mexico? But how?

\- - -

Aztec temples? Don't you mean Maya? The Aztecs are in Peru.

\- - -

Yes. I get them mixed up sometimes too. So was she visiting them too?

\- - -

But why did she need to borrow money from you?

\- - -

Yes. I know you have to be careful. And she's so rich too. Whoever took it must have made off with a packet of money.

\- - -

As much as that? Wow! So she invited you to the premiere performance in London?

\- - -

I'll bet it was.

\- - -

Lucky you, meeting all those other celebrities too.

\- - -

Box 58 *continued*

- -

Advanced

Oh, no, just small ones. We caught them just after the monsoon rains started.

Sorry? No. We couldn't find anywhere to leave them. We've still got them with us.

Yes. Here in the flat. Erm, in fact I was wondering if we could leave them here tonight. Do you think your mother would mind?

No, nothing like last time. I promise.

Well, we need the bathtub really. The kitchen sink's too small.

Well, yes, they are small … but not that small. And we wouldn't want them to crawl out.

Can you? That would be great. Can you call me back and let me know what she says?

No, I promise you it won't happen again. Nothing like last time. And these are not even poisonous. Really harmless …

Box 59

A: What are you writing?
B:
A: Not writing?
B:
A: Why not?
B:
A: Doesn't stop others … Written out?
B: Yes. Now what are YOU writing?
A:

EDWARD BOND *Bingo*

Note
This is a useful activity for developing intuitive anticipation of the missing language.

10.6 Conflict

Aim	To use a scenario involving conflict to develop a dramatic improvisation
Focus	Vocabulary will depend on the specific scenarios set up; expressions of accusation, apology, negotiation, etc.
Level	Intermediate and above
Time	One class hour
Preparation	You need cards or slips of paper outlining a number of conflict situations. Box 60 provides some examples.

Procedure
1 Put students in pairs. Explain that they will each have a conflict situation. They have to use this as the starting point for an improvisation in which they try to resolve the situation – peacefully if possible. They should start with rational arguments. Only if this fails, should they move to a more emotional level.
2 Distribute the cards, one per pair. Allow 15 minutes for discussion of the situation and for a first run-through of the improvisation. Each member of a pair should play both roles, before finally deciding on who will play A and B.
3 Each pair joins another pair. They perform their improvisations for each other. The object here is for pairs to offer each other constructive criticism to help them improve their improvisations.
4 Each pair now joins a different pair. They again perform their 'improved' improvisations for each other.
5 In a whole-class session, ask for one or two pairs to perform their improvisations.

Follow-on
If you have access to a camcorder, try making videos of some of the better improvisations (but make sure you get students' agreement first). These videos can be kept in your materials archive and then be used as input to classes with other groups.

Variation
Students work in groups of five or six to work on the conflict situations in Box 61.

Box 60

You invited your best friend to your birthday party last month. He has not invited you to his party next week. You have bought him a nice present. You meet him in the street and he does not mention his birthday.

Your parents want you to babysit for them this Saturday, but you have already arranged to go to a party. It is very important to you.

You and your sister (brother) share a car. She (he) wants to use it tonight to take her (his) latest boyfriend (girlfriend) to a party. You need it to get to a late business meeting in the next town. (There is no public transport late at night.)

You are a teenage girl who wants to go to Thailand for a holiday alone. Your mother is against the idea.

You and your new wife live in a very small flat in a city centre. She wants a dog as a pet. You are against it.

You recently started a new job with a high salary, where the emphasis is on loyalty to the company. You have promised to take your wife and two young children away for the weekend (for the first time in over a year). Now your boss wants you to work this Saturday on an important contract.

Your wife (husband) wants her (his) aged mother to come and live with you in your small flat. You are against the idea.

Note

It is important that pairs discuss the situation before they start the improvisation, so that they have some thoughts about the kinds of arguments they might use or have used against them. Too much discussion will spoil the spontaneity of reactions, however.

See also Chapter 11, *Warming up*, *Improvisation* and *Rehearsal*.

Box 61

An old lady is having a long personal conversation with the clerk at the village post office. There is a queue of busy people waiting behind her.

In a non-smoking railway carriage, a tough-looking young man is smoking.

You work on the night shift and need to sleep during the day. Every afternoon for the last week, the neighbours' children have played football against the wall of your house. They have just woken you up – again.

You are on an aeroplane. You have asked the flight attendant several times to bring you a drink. She has brought drinks to other passengers near you but not to you.

10.7 Tension

Aim	To use a situation involving tension to develop a dramatic improvisation
Focus	Vocabulary will depend on the situation chosen; intonation to express emotional charge; language of discussion and evaluation
Level	Intermediate and above
Time	Two class hours
Preparation	Prepare a number of cards or slips of paper with brief descriptions of situations involving tension. Box 62 provides some examples.

Procedure

First class hour

1 Explain that each group of five students will be given a situation involving tension. Write one of the situations in Box 62 on the board. Elicit suggestions from students as to how the situation might develop and what the outcome might be. Discuss with them who the characters might be, how they might act and the things they might say.

2 Distribute one situation card to each group of five. Allow 15 minutes for discussion of the situation and of characters, actions and language.

3 Collect feedback on this in a whole-class session.

4   Allow groups another 20 minutes to produce a written version of their situation in the form of a short playscript.

5   Each group exchanges its script with another group.

Second class hour

6   Groups first try to improve the script they have been given. You should give help as necessary.

7   Groups rehearse the script and perform it for the whole class.

Box 62

The bus is late. You and your friends have an important exam at school. It takes 30 minutes to walk to school. The bus still has not come 30 minutes before the start of the exam.

Your parents are late home. It is nearly midnight. You and your small brother are alone in the house.

You are passengers in a hijacked aircraft. One passenger suddenly has a heart attack.

You are travelling in a strange country with your friends. Your car has broken down at night on a lonely desert road. Another car stops. A man gets out. He has a gun.

You are all trapped in a lift: suddenly someone smells gas.

You work in a big company which has been losing money. You have all been called to a meeting. You know that some of you may be told you have been dismissed.

You have been working abroad for a year. When you come back to your house, you find some strangers are living there.

You have 'neighbours from hell'. They make noise until late at night. They throw rubbish into your garden. They are aggressive to everyone. You need to get to the hospital but they have parked their car blocking your driveway.

When you invited your best friend to a beach party he/she told you that he/she was busy with a meeting at work. You change your plans and go to a restaurant with some other friends instead. You see your best friend happily enjoying dinner with someone you have never seen before.

Notes

1 Step 1 is important in guiding students on how to go about developing the action and the language.
2 The editing stage is also important both for generating ideas and for improving language. It is always easier to make improvements to other people's work than to our own.

See also Chapter 11, *Warming up, Improvisation* and *Rehearsal.*

10.8 The hole

Aim	To develop a short dramatic sketch on the basis of a simple scenario
Focus	Vocabulary will depend on the scenario selected; language of discussion, evaluation
Level	Lower-Intermediate and above
Time	One class hour
Preparation	Either write the information in Box 63 on the board or make copies of it (one per group of five).

Box 63

The event/setting

Just outside a village in the town of Brobnag, a deep hole appears overnight. A small child discovers it in the morning and runs to inform the police.

The characters

- the child
- the police chief
- the mayor (a politician)
- a scientist
- an artist
- a practical joker
- a businessman
- a pessimist
- a retired army colonel

© CAMBRIDGE UNIVERSITY PRESS 2005

Procedure

1 Students work in groups of five. Distribute the copies of Box 63 to each group (or ask them to see the information on the board).
2 Allow five minutes for groups to decide on which five characters they will choose to include in their dramatisation. Each of them takes one part.
3 Allow another 20 minutes for groups to work out a dramatisation with the following scenes:
   • The characters gather round the hole: their first reactions.
   • A town meeting where they discuss what to do about the hole.
   • The final solution.
4 Each group performs its dramatisation for another group. They compare notes.
5 Conduct a whole-class feedback. Some groups may be asked to reperform for the whole class.

Variations

1 Students work in pairs with this scenario:
   Two people are sitting at a table. There is an apple in the middle of the table. It is the last apple they have. They are both hungry but neither can just grab the apple and eat it. How will they solve the problem?
2 Students can work in groups as large as ten. They develop a dramatisation, with words, of this scenario:
   Two people are looking intently at a spot somewhere high above them in a shopping mall. People begin to gather, looking up too, talking excitedly to each other. When a group has formed, the two people slip quietly away.
3 Students work in threes on this scenario:
   Two travellers arrive at a customs post. They have to wait ages before the officer sees them. By then it is closing time. The officer tells them to come back the next day.
   Next morning the officer tells them they need to get a special document from the office in the next town. They go back to the town, rushing from office to office. By the time they get the document and arrive back at the frontier, it is closing again.
   Next morning, they go early to the frontier with all their documents. The officer tells them that they no longer need the document from the previous day. Regulations have changed. Now they need a different document ...

Note

Obviously, students at a more advanced stage will be able to develop more sophisticated dialogue, but even lower-level students can come up with good (usually humorous) ideas. You will almost certainly need to be on hand to help out with language.

See also Chapter 11, *Improvisation* and *Rehearsal*.

10.9 Role reversal

Aim	To develop an improvised script based on the reversal of normal roles
Focus	Vocabulary will depend on the situation chosen; interactive dialogue structure, especially how to interrupt, make suggestions, persuade; language of discussion and evaluation
Level	Upper-Intermediate–Advanced
Time	Two class hours
Preparation	Prepare cards or slips of paper containing brief outlines of role reversals. Box 64 provides some examples.

Procedure

1 You will need to explain the concept of role-reversal, e.g. when a parent becomes a child, and the child a parent. Discuss how such a change might take place in a dramatic episode: the child might suggest an improvement to an instruction the parent has given; this goes on until it is the child who is giving instructions to the parent.

2 Students work in groups of three. Give each group one of the cards you have prepared. Allow at least 20 minutes for students to discuss how the scene could be worked out in terms of the language needed, possible actions and props. They should write this out as a script with directions as necessary.

3 Conduct whole-class feedback on the suggestions, correcting language and suggesting improvements as necessary.

4 Groups exchange their situations. Each group then tries to improve the script it has received (if necessary, this can be done as homework).

5 In the next class, allow groups 15 minutes to rehearse their original, corrected scripts. Each group then performs its role-reversal skit for the whole class (in large classes, each group can perform for one other group). Leave time for class feedback on each skit.

Box 64

In a doctor's surgery, a window cleaner intervenes in the consultation, giving advice to the patient. By the end, he has taken over from the doctor – wearing the doctor's white jacket and sitting in his chair.

- -

A passerby in the street intervenes when a policeman is arresting a thief. In the end, it is the thief and passerby who arrest the policeman.

- -

A politician is giving a speech. A member of the audience begins by interrupting with questions. By the end, the questioner has taken over the platform and the politician is in the audience.

- -

The accused in a trial begins to ask questions of the lawyer (or the judge). In the end, it is the lawyer (or judge) who is in the witness box, and the accused who is judging the case (see *Prisoner and Judge*, poem by Ian Serailler).

- -

In a department store, a shop assistant is trying to persuade a shopper to buy something. Another shopper comes along. In the end, the second shopper has persuaded the shop assistant to buy the goods, and takes the money.

- -

In a restaurant, the waiter becomes so engrossed in recommending items from the menu that he sits down with the diners. In the end, he is served the food by one of the diners.

- -

A husband and wife are enjoying an evening at home. There is a knock at the door. It is a person selling a special new gadget. They invite the salesperson in. In the end, the salesperson has taken the husband's (or wife's) place, leaving them to go out into the street to sell the gadget.

Notes

1   It is important that students get the point that this is a kind of surrealist activity, where the normal rules of social behaviour do not hold. The fact that these are implausible situations is the whole point. Once students understand the humorous possibilities of role-reversal, however, they usually exploit them with gusto.

2   As indicated in Focus above, students will need to master ways of breaking in to the ongoing discourse. Useful language will include: *Excuse me. Just a minute. Could I just make a suggestion? Could I say*

something? *Why don't you …? Maybe it would be better if … I'll tell you what we could do. Why don't I … and why don't you …?* It is language like this which is crucial to the crossover point in the exchange of roles.

3 For classes with a literary interest, you can point out that this device has been used by a number of writers, including George Orwell (1945) in *Animal Farm*, Mark Twain (1882) in *The Prince and the Pauper* and R. L. Stevenson (1886) in *Dr Jekyll and Mr Hyde*.

See also Chapter 11, *Improvisation* and Rehearsal.

10.10 A real bargain

Aim	To act out a short playscript
Focus	Appropriate pronunciation, stress and intonation
Level	Intermediate and above
Time	20 minutes in one class; homework time out of class; one class hour
Preparation	Choose a fairly simple and short sketch with not more than three or four characters. Box 65 provides an example.

Procedure

1 Distribute the playscript a week before you intend to use it. Tell students that, for homework, they will be preparing to act one of the roles in the play. Put them in groups of three and let them decide who will play which role.

2 Read through the script with students. Pay special attention to stress and intonation. Many of the utterances are quite emphatic. You can exaggerate the intonation patterns to help students get the point.

3 In the class a week later, give groups ten minutes to run through their sketch together. Then ask each group to perform it for the class.

4 After each performance, suggest improvements to the intonation students have used, and encourage them to make suggestions, too.

Notes

1 Though you are not rehearsing a full performance, you can still encourage students to add movement and gesture as they read their parts.

2 Intonation is notoriously difficult to master. If you have access to one or more native, or very proficient, speakers, ask them to help by making an audio recording of the sketch. This will act as a model for students. If you have a native-speaker teaching assistant, this is the time to use him/her to the full!

Box 65

*Sunday evening. A highroad jammed with cars. In a car, a man and woman are
talking.*
Sue: Why didn't we stop at that snackbar we passed five miles back?
Bob: Oh, stop complaining.
Sue: I'm not complaining. I'm hungry, that's all.
Bob: Me too. I'm sure we'll find something soon.
Sue: What? Out here in the middle of nowhere! You must be joking! You really get
on my nerves sometimes.
Bob: Oh, shut up! (*Pause*) Hey, wait a minute. Look over there. What about that?
*He jumps out of the car and runs over to an old peasant sitting on a wall. The
peasant is eating something. It is obviously delicious.*
Bob: Excuse me … That looks really delicious. Have you got any more?
Man: More what? *Goes on eating.*
Bob: More of those pies – like the one you're eating.
Man: Sorry.
Bob: Are you sure? What about that one in the paper bag over there?
Man: Sorry. I can't let you have that. I'm keeping it to eat later for my supper.
Bob: Look, I'll give you five pounds for it, OK?
Man: I told you – I can't sell it. Sorry.
Bob: OK, I'll make that seven pounds. Try and help me out – we're starving.
Man: Well …
Bob gives him the money and takes the pie back to the car.
Bob: Here you are, darling. I told you we'd find something.
Sue: Mmm. Smells delicious. *Takes a bite.* Oh yes. It's really tasty.
Bob: Hey. Leave some for me! *Takes a bite too.* Mmm. You're right. It's really
good.
Sue: You're so clever, darling …
*The traffic begins to move again. The old peasant goes behind a wall and takes
another pie from his basket hidden there.*
Man: Idiots! Anyway, I've only got a few left now. It's been a good day's business. It
shouldn't take long to get rid of the rest of them. Here comes another one
now!! I wonder how much he'll be willing to pay?

ALAN MALEY

© Cambridge University Press 2005

3   There are a number of collections of short plays specially written for
EFL/ESL learners (see Bibliography). One of the best is Case and Wilson
(1995a; 1995b), *English Sketches* (two books at two levels). The sketches
I have found most effective and popular with students have been: *The*

Ticket Inspector; *Gussett and Rose*; *Mr Jones*; *The Dentist*; *The Bank*; *Gerry Brown's Driving Test*; *Giovanni's Café*. This collection is doubly useful as it has accompanying audio cassettes.

10.11 Real theatre scripts

Aim	To introduce students to authentic drama scripts written for performance in real theatres
Focus	Appropriate pronunciation, stress, intonation and voice quality
Level	Intermediate and above
Time	At least one class hour
Preparation	You will need to find and reproduce either a complete short play or a self-standing extract. You need enough copies for one between every two students. Box 66 provides an example of a short extract from Harold Pinter's play *The Dumb Waiter*. In this play, two hired killers are waiting in a deserted room for their instructions. They are tense and nervous. They have been arguing about football teams.

Procedure

1   Distribute the scripts, one for every pair of students. Allow a few minutes for them to read through the script.

2   Go through the script with them. What do they notice? What is the relationship between the two characters? Who is more dominant? What do you think they look like? Why does one character ask questions to which the answers are obvious, e.g. *What's that?*, when he can see it's an envelope? Why does one character say there is nothing in the envelope, when it is still sealed? Why does one character never seem to understand anything the first time? What is the reason for putting matches in the envelope? Who pushed the envelope under the door? What is the atmosphere like in this scene? What do you think will happen next?

3   Students work in groups of four. Distribute two copies of the script per group. In each group, two students will prepare a dramatised reading. The other two will be directors of the play. They should actively offer advice on the way the lines are to be spoken, any movements, facial expressions, etc. Allow 15 minutes for this.

4   Each group takes turns to perform the script for the whole class. Elicit feedback after each group's performance. How effective was it? How could it be improved? How different were the groups' performances?

Box 66

An envelope slides under the door, right. Gus sees it. He stands, looking at it.
Gus: Ben,
Ben: Away. They're playing away.
Gus: Ben, look here,
Ben: What?
Gus: Look.
Ben turns his head and sees the envelope.
Ben: What's that?
Gus: I don't know.
Ben: Where did it come from?
Gus: Under the door.
Ben: Well, what is it?
Gus: I don't know.
They stare at it.
Ben: Pick it up.
Gus: What do you mean?
Ben: Pick it up!
Gus slowly moves towards it, bends and picks it up.
Ben: What is it?
Gus: An envelope.
Ben: Is there anything in it?
Gus: No.
Ben: Is it sealed?
Gus: Yes.
Ben: Open it.
Gus: What?
Ben: Open it!
Gus opens it and looks inside.
Ben: What's in it?
Gus empties twelve matches into his hand.
Gus: Matches.

HAROLD PINTER *The Dumb Waiter*

Follow-on
1   In the next class, choose another similar script for two actors. Students work in the same groups. This time, those who acted become the directors; the directors become the actors.

2   If students enjoyed this extract, let them read (act?) the continuation of this scene or perhaps the whole play (see Chapter 11 Into Performance).

Variation
Using the same script, and working in the same groups of four, students try to flesh out the dialogue by adding lines to the very minimal utterances of the two characters.

Notes
1   Step 2 is important. Students need help to 'get inside the skin' of the text. They cannot be expected to empathise with it immediately. This is especially true of contemporary scripts, such as this one, which is a kind of 'theatre of the absurd'. Much of what happens in scripts of this kind is going on below the surface, e.g. the vaguely menacing atmosphere brought about by unexplained happenings, the way one character compensates for his own fear by bullying the other, etc.
2   Step 4 is equally important in helping students to realise how many different ways there are of speaking these very simple-looking lines.

See also Chapter 11, *Warming up, Improvisation* and *Rehearsal.*

11 Into performance

For many people, doing drama work and putting on a play are the same thing: 'Why do all those activities if it doesn't lead to a finished product? What's the point?' We hope that the answer to that question is by now obvious. Drama activities have a value in contributing to the language-learning process quite apart from any finished product they may lead to. Yet it is undeniable that there is real value in putting on real performances – for a real audience. This option may not be open to everyone, however. Why not?

- Preparing a performance requires a great deal of time. Not every class will have enough time available, either in terms of class time or extra time outside class.
- It is difficult to do with large classes. One of the benefits of putting on performances is that everyone in the group can have an active role, even if this is not as an actor (see below). But in a large class, this is simply not possible.
- Both teacher and students have to be motivated enough to cheerfully take on all the hard work and setbacks involved in a real production. Such commitment is relatively rare, sometimes for very good reasons, such as heavy teaching loads.

Nonetheless, it is possible to settle for less than a full-length, elaborately costumed, public performance. A short sketch, if properly rehearsed, can still share many of the advantages of 'performance'. Even a rehearsed reading is better than nothing. What then are the main benefits of putting on a play as a project?

Benefits from performance

- There is a high degree of linguistic reinforcement. The number of purposeful repetitions of the script involve students in 'deep processing' of the language in a way which is usually impossible in normal lessons.
- Repeated rehearsal allows time for intensive work on pronunciation, especially supra-segmental features such as stress, rhythm and intonation. In class there is rarely enough time for this kind of

concentrated attention to these features. Students, knowing they will be 'on show', will go to incredible lengths to get it right.

- Increasing familiarity with the text (by both actors and everyone else involved with the play) leads to greater fluency in oral delivery.
- Focus is firmly on meaning rather than form. This increases understanding of the importance of both linguistic co-text and situational context.
- There is scope for intensive, even heated, discussion at every stage in the production: discussion of the themes embodied in the piece; discussion of how to present given scenes: where people should stand, how they should move, etc.; discussion of how some lines should be spoken to achieve the desired effect. This is focus on meaning with a vengeance.
- There is a pay-off in terms of self-esteem. 'We did it! We really did!' This is true even for the non-actors. Everyone involved has had a hand in the success of the play project. Everyone involved takes a share of the good feelings they experience as a group; and increased self-esteem is often reflected in increased motivation to go on learning English in its more mundane manifestations.
- Putting on a play opens students' minds to the dramatic genre. They begin to understand how plays work, as verbal artefacts, as spectacle, as a reflection (or a critique) of cultural and social norms. This is in itself a valuable educational process, which has to be experienced; it is much less effective if it is simply explained.

How to tackle the 'Play project'

There is no right way to put on a play. But there are a number of factors which always need attention. In what follows, we shall make some suggestions, make reference to activities already described earlier in this book, and offer a few new activities to speed the project on its way.

Selecting a play

Criteria for selection will always be subjective to a degree, and will also depend partly on whether the play is a full-length production to be performed publicly or a less ambitious short play or sketch to be performed within the class, or for others in the school.

- *Length* It is clearly better to start with relatively short, one-act plays or sketches (see the suggestions at the end of this section).

- *Number of characters* If you want to involve everyone, then plays with more rather than fewer characters are to be preferred. However, if it is to be a modest production in class, with several groups working simultaneously on the same play, it may be better to choose plays with two or three characters only.
- *Language difficulty* This will be a major consideration. Plays containing long and involved speeches, complex syntax and difficult or archaic vocabulary would normally not be suitable.
- *Paralinguistic features* In most cases, it will be better to choose plays with plenty of scope for movement and opportunities for using body-language rather than those where the characters become no more than 'talking heads'.
- *Familiarity/Accessibility* Clearly it will be best to avoid plays with an over-intellectual content, requiring an advanced understanding of the foreign (i.e. English) culture or subculture, or with high literary pretensions. The theme and content and the ways they are addressed need to be relatively close to the students' level.
- *Relevance* It will be better to choose plays with subject matter the students perceive as relevant to their own lives. This may often mean choosing humorous plays – but not inevitably so. For instance, *When the Wind Blows* by Raymond Briggs (1982, Penguin), a cartoon book easily adaptable for performance, and concerning nuclear war and its aftermath, is perceived by many students as highly relevant.
- *Self-contained* This refers largely to the use of extracts from full-length plays. It is best to use extracts which are complete in themselves and can stand alone.
- *Low resource* The best plays for use with students will be those requiring relatively few props, changes of scenery or lighting changes. Keep it simple!
- *Spin-off value* Some teachers will be looking for plays which offer them the opportunity to develop language-related activities which arise naturally from the play, e.g. a play might spark off the design of a questionnaire to do with family violence, or cruelty to animals, etc.; or it may lend itself to creative writing of poems, etc. Of course, many plays would fall into this category, but not all teachers take equal note of them.
- *Interest* The play has to be interesting for the students concerned. There is nothing worse than plugging away at a 'contemporary critical success', or a 'classic of the British theatre', if it turns the students off. It would be wise to associate the students with the final choice of play, by offering them perhaps three possible choices.

Getting to know the text

- Start by giving some background information about the play, its author, the circumstances in which it was written (if these are known), when it was first performed, whether it is well known or not, etc. Say what you like about it and why you think it is an effective play. (Some of this may well have already been discussed in coming to a decision on which play to select but it does no harm to remind students.) Then briefly describe the characters and the action.

- In order to discuss plays, students will need some basic theatrical vocabulary, so part of getting to know the play may be learning this vocabulary. It will comprise items such as: *text, actor, character, role, action, comedy/tragedy/farce, act/scene, entrance/exit, upstage/ downstage*, etc.

- Take a key scene from the play and show students how they can 'interrogate' it. What do the words say? What do they mean? Do they mean what they say or is there a hidden meaning if we read 'between the lines'? It will be best to do this with the whole group, at least to start with, until they gain enough confidence to do it independently in smaller groups.

- Show students how to contextualise the script. They need to discuss *where* it takes place, *who* the characters are, *when* the action happens, *why* people do what they do or say what they say.

- This contextualisation will lead naturally into a discussion of character and the relationships between characters, their intentions and motivations, their roles and status. It will be helpful for them to build up through discussion a detailed impression of each character: age, personality, appearance, occupation, mood, etc. This will help them in building the character as a real person, who will grow out of the words on the page. One way of making this more challenging is to remove all characters' names and any stage directions. All students have to work with is the dialogue. What can they tell about the characters only from what they say?

- If the play does not have stage directions, ask students to supply them. If it does have stage directions, blank them out and let students supply their own. This activity forces students to visualise how the actors will move, their way of speaking, their mood and manner, etc. Here is a short example:

Sir Jasper: Come in, my dear. What kept you so long? I've been waiting for you since midday.

Susan:	I'm, I'm so, so sorry, I erm, I was delayed at the, the bank.
Sir J:	At the bank? But it's a public holiday today. The banks are closed!
Susan:	Oh, is it? Are they? I mean, maybe I am getting it mixed up with yesterday. Erm … Oh dear, I don't think I feel very well. Can you get me a glass of water? Pleeeease.

With stage directions added:

(Sir Jasper is a middle-aged man who has invited a young lady to his apartment. He has been waiting in his luxury apartment for over three hours. He has a very jealous personality.)

Sir Jasper:	*(Forces himself to sound relaxed)* Come in, my dear. *(Increasingly impatient and irritated)* What kept you so long? *(Speaking very loudly)* I've been waiting for you since midday.
Susan:	*(A very attractive young lady. She arrives flustered and seems uneasy)* I'm, I'm so, so sorry. *(She desperately tries to think up an excuse)* I erm, I was delayed at the bank.
Sir Jasper:	*(Very suspicious, and irritable)* At the bank? *(He knows she is lying)* But it's a public holiday today. The banks are closed!
Susan:	*(She is now very embarrassed and doesn't know what to say)* Oh, is it? Are they? I mean, maybe I'm getting it mixed up with yesterday. Erm … *(She realises this is a very poor excuse and tries another tactic. She pretends to feel faint. She speaks as a weak and helpless girl, appealing for his help)* Oh dear, I don't think I feel very well. Can you get me a glass of water? Pleeeease. *(She falls backward into an armchair and begins to fan her face with her handkerchief)*

ALAN MALEY *Oh Sir Jasper, do not touch me!*

- Choose a single scene, and ask students to read it through together. Assign roles for a first reading. Then change them around for a second and third reading, so that students begin to get a feel for how easy or difficult the lines are to speak. Let men and women swap roles, so that they are speaking as a member of the opposite sex.

Warming up

Before every session of working on the playscript, organise some simple warm-up activities. These should cover relaxation, breathing, body work, voice work and group bonding. You can find suitable activities in Chapter 1 Getting ready and Chapter 4 Working with the voice:

- relaxation, see pages 70–71
- breathing, see pages 73–75
- bodywork, see pages 71–73
- voicework, see pages 75–78
- group bonding, see pages 7–18.

Improvisation

Once students are a little familiar with the script, having done some of the activities from *Getting to know the text* on pages 232–3 and having warmed up, let them try some of the improvisation activities below. Here they are being invited to 'play around' with material from the play as a preliminary to rehearsal, where they will be bound by the script.

- Take a key word from the script, e.g. *Please* or *the bank* or *closed* from the *Sir Jasper* extract above. Students mime the word for each other, in pairs. They then add words which come to mind in association with it e.g.:

    Please don't be angry. Please get me a drink. Please come and sit here. Please let me sit down. Please let's talk about something else.

- Take a speech act, such as apologising, requesting help, accusing, etc. from the script and ask them, in pairs, to improvise a short scene, first in mime, then adding their own words. The more imaginative their ideas, the better. Here is an example for the speech act making excuses, from the *Sir Jasper*.

    Oh, am I late? Oh is that really the time? I'm so sorry, I got stopped for speeding. I know I'm late but my mother called me over to look after the dog while she went to the doctor's. Oh dear, I know I'm late. I'm ever so sorry. I got locked in the loo at Waterloo station. etc.

- Take a fragment of the script and ask students, in pairs, to vary the way they speak it in the following ways:
    - varying their gesture and movement as they speak it
    - varying the status of the two speakers, i.e. the one with higher status adopts lower status, and vice versa
    - varying tone of voice: angry, disappointed, suspicious, friendly, etc.

– varying the general atmosphere between the two speakers: relaxed, threatening, tense, etc.

At this stage, it does not matter if students have not learnt the lines perfectly, as long as they convey the gist.

- Give students an outline of a scene, and ask them to improvise what would be said and how (including gesture and movement), e.g.:

  A: You are a young girl. You've just been seeing your young boyfriend. This has made you late for your appointment with your middle-aged, rich lover. You are worried because you know he gets very jealous.

  B: You are a middle-aged man waiting for your attractive young girlfriend. She is very late. You suspect she may have been seeing someone else. You do not like that.

  When students have improvised with their partner, they exchange roles and repeat the improvisation. They change partners and do it again. They change partners once more but this time, they enact the scene silently, simply mouthing the words and conveying meaning through facial expression and gesture.

See also Chapters 8, 9 and 10. These chapters all have a wealth of activities which can be used in the improvisation stage of a production.

Rehearsal

This is when students really get started on the script. You (or the director, if it is one of the students) will need to start thinking about casting (i.e. who will play which role?). At the outset, however, it is better not to cast too early. Let everyone be involved as actors in the early stages, even though later they may have non-acting jobs (see *Involving everyone* on page 237). Below are some ways of approaching the script in rehearsal. Do not forget that, before every rehearsal, students will need to do some warming up, as in *Warming up* on page 234.

- Read the script in scenes (or in sections which seem to make sense as wholes). At first, let students read the text seated. Then standing. Then change roles two or three times. This is when the director is looking for a good 'fit' between the role and the actor who will play it.
- Read the script in scenes (or sections), but this time, add movement. What does the script suggest, or prescribe, in terms of movement? It will be useful to encourage plenty of discussion at this stage. Often students come up with highly original suggestions about movement.

How, for example, does a character enter? Running, walking, erect, stooping, etc.? At this stage, it will be good to switch roles between different students.

- Assign roles provisionally and ask students to learn their part for a scene or two. Then play the scene without movement. The focus will be on different ways of speaking the script, varying sentence stress, intonation, tone of voice, volume, pace, pausing, etc. for the best effect. Again, encourage discussion.

- Continue playing the scene but add movement. How well do the movements work at this stage? Again, encourage discussion. The production emerges partly as a result of consensus being reached between all those involved. Try to restrain your teacherly role of telling them which way is best! Sometimes, what emerges from discussion and trial and error is far more effective than what you may have had in mind at the outset.

- Run through the same scene but without the words, silently. Students act out their roles in mime and movement alone.

- Repeat the scene. Students have learnt their (provisional) parts. This time, give each student a prop of some kind: a hat, a walking stick, a telephone, a pocket calculator, a book, etc. and let them see how they can incorporate their prop into the scene as they speak it.

- Again, having learnt their parts, let students perform but wearing masks (see 5.10 Masks). What difference does this make to the way they speak their parts? A more extreme form of this activity is to blindfold the actors. What effect does this have on the way they react to each other, the way they move?

- There will come a point when the director has to decide who will play each role. Those chosen as actors can be asked to write an autobiographical statement about themselves in role. Where were they (i.e. the character they are acting) born? What were their parents like? How did they perform at school? When did they first fall in love? Out of love? etc. These autobiographies can be used as the basis for interviews. Students who have not been chosen as actors can interview the actors about their lives, about how they would react in certain situations, etc.

See also Chapters 4, 8, 9 and 10. These chapters all contain activities suitable for use in the rehearsal stage of the production.

Involving everyone

It is really important that everyone feels they have a stake in the production, that, without them, the production would be less effective. Usually, after a few rehearsals, people seem to drift naturally towards certain roles; and some are clearly not attracted by an acting role at all. The important thing is that everyone has a job. What jobs are there?

- *Director* If it is a first-time production, this role had better be done by you, the teacher. If the group does more than one production, one of the more proficient students may be entrusted with this role in a later production, under your guidance.
- *Stage manager* Responsible for all aspects of what takes place on stage: scene changes, coordinating lighting, ensuring actors get on at the right time, etc.
- *Lighting and sound* These may be minimal (and unless you have access to proper theatre lighting and sound equipment, they should be!). However, even minimal lighting and sound need someone to operate effectively at the right moment.
- *Scenery and props* Even though there may be minimal scenery and props (things like telephones, etc. which are needed by the actors), someone has to be responsible for producing or acquiring them.
- *Costumes* It is best to avoid elaborate costumes, unless you have a big budget. But someone has to make sure that each actor has what is needed at the time it is needed.
- *Makeup* You need to decide how elaborate makeup should be. Students usually love to appear in stage makeup, so even if it may not be essential, it may be worth doing. There is usually at least one student who just loves to apply the makeup!
- *The actors* By this stage, you will have tried out a number of people for each role and decided on a final list.
- *The understudies* Understudies are actors who have to learn their parts just as well as the main actors. However, understudies are only called upon to act if one or more of the leading actors is sick or unable to go on stage.
- *The prompter* This person has to know the play and the particular production inside out. It is their role to prompt any actor who has obviously forgotten lines or completely 'dried up'.
- *Programme notes* For this, it may be best to choose a student who is interested in writing rather than acting. Programme notes usually include

information about the play itself, the author and brief notes on the players.

- *Publicity* If the play is to be performed for the outside public (or even for the whole school), someone will need to design posters or fliers, possibly set up a website to advertise ther play, organise tickets, etc.

A few practical considerations

- Before embarking on a drama project, check that you have the support of your school or institution, and, where applicable, of parents. You may also need to enlist the support or agreement of colleagues, whose own work may be affected by rehearsals, etc. Check, too, that you have a budget to cover whatever costs are involved (costumes, makeup, scenery, etc. and even such things as snacks and drinks for the breaks!).
- How long should the process take from beginning to end, from choosing the script to the first night? Much will depend on local circumstances, and on how many times a week the group can meet for preparation and rehearsal. For a short sketch, like one of those in Case and Wilson (1995a, 1995b) referred to on page 225 it should be possible to put on a performance with minimal props and equipment in two weeks, if the group meets at least once a day. For a longer play with more complex requirements, a month to six weeks might be enough. The main thing is not to allow so much time that the whole thing becomes a chore and a bore.
- Discipline: you need to make it clear from the outset that the drama project will be a lot of fun, and bring about a lot of learning, but only if everyone plays by the rules. Set out clearly the schedule of meetings (especially those which will take place outside class hours), who will be needed for each one, and the time they will start and finish. It will be best if you negotiate this schedule rather than imposing it, since students will then feel a degree of ownership over it. Make it clear that everyone needs to be punctual and to cooperate. Start and end rehearsals on time to show that you mean business. You can be firm without being dictatorial.
- The role of the teacher: apart from ensuring that everything is well planned and carried out in a disciplined but friendly way, the teacher will be a constant reference-point for matters of language and information, a constant peacemaker when disputes blow up (and they do), a constant source of encouragement for everyone. If you decide to take on this role, you will need all the reserves of good-humour, patience, resilience in the face of difficulty, and as much sheer grit and perseverance as you can muster. Good luck! Let the show begin!

Some possible sources for plays

Applicant Harold Pinter
Over the Wall James Saunders
(Both in Shackleton, M. [ed] [1985] *Double Act*, Edward Arnold.)
Five One-Act Plays Wolf Mankowitz (1964), Evans Bros. Ltd.
Dog Accident James Saunders
The (15 minute) Dogg's Troupe Hamlet Tom Stoppard
(Both in Berman, E. D. (ed) (1979) *10 of the Best*, London: InterAction Imprint.)
Publishers specialising in playscripts include:
Samuel French, London
Methuen & Co. Ltd, London
Faber & Faber, London.

Bibliography

Books on Drama in Education

Barker, C. (1977) *Theatre Games*, Methuen.
Bowskill, D. (1973) *Acting and Stagecraft Made Simple*, W. H. Allen.
Brook, P. (1972) *The Empty Space*, Penguin.
Challen, J. (1973) *Drama Casebook: A Chronicle of Experience*, Methuen Educational Ltd.
Frost, A. and Yarrow, R. (1990) *Improvisation in Drama*, Macmillan.
Hodgson, J. (1977) *The Uses of Drama*, Methuen.
Hodgson, J. and Richards, E. (1967) *Improvisation*, Methuen.
Johnstone, K. (1981) *IMPRO: Improvisation and the Theatre*, Methuen.
Johnstone, K. (1999) *Impro for Story-tellers*, Routledge.
McCaslin, N. (1996) *Creative Drama in the Classroom and Beyond*, New York: Longman.
Maley, A. (1984) 'A roomful of human beings', *Singapore RELC Guidelines*, 5, 2.
Rittenberg, M. and Kreitzer, P. (1981) *English Through Drama*, Hayward Calif: Alemany Press.
Seely, J. (1976) *In Context: Language and Drama in the Secondary School*, OUP.
Spolin, V. (1966) *Improvisation for the Theatre*, Pitman.
Verriour, P. (1994) *In Role: Teaching and Learning Dramatically*, Scarborough, Ontario: Pippin Publishing.
Wagner, B. J. (1979) *Dorothy Heathcote – Drama as a Learning Medium*, Hutchinson.
Way, B. (1967) *Development through Drama*, Longman.
Wessels, C. (1987) *Drama*, OUP.

Source materials for activities

Crystal, D. (1998) *Language Play*, Penguin.
Hoper, C. *et al.* (1976) *Awareness Games*, New York: St Martin's Press.
Jones, K. (1982) *Simulations in Language Teaching*, CUP.

Maley, A. (1999) 'Choral speaking', *English Teaching Professional*, 12, July.

Pfeiffer, J. W. and Jones, J. E. (1973) *A Handbook of Structured Experiences for Human Relations Training*, Vols I to VI, La Jolla: Calif. University Associates.

Moskowitz, G. (1978) *Caring and Sharing in the Foreign Language Classroom*, Newbury House.

Phillips, S. (1999) *Drama with Children*, OUP.

Porter-Ladousse, G. (1987) *Role-Play*, OUP.

Ratliff, G. L. (1999) *Introduction to Reader's Theatre*, Colorado Springs: Meriwether Press.

Scher, A. and Verrall, C. (1975) *100 Ideas for Drama*, Heinemann.

Simon, S. B. *et al.* (1995) *Values Clarification*, New York: Warner Books.

Ur, P. (1981) *Discussions that Work*, CUP.

Wright, A. *et al.* (1980) *Games for Language Learning*, CUP.

Wright, A. (1995) *Storytelling with Children*, OUP.

Wright, A. (1997) *Creating Stories with Children*, OUP.

Source materials for short poems, etc.

Ahlberg, A. (1989) *Heard in the Playground*, Viking.

Clement, F. (1974) *Word Spinning*, London: Evans.

Dahl, R. (1989) *Rhyme Stew*, Penguin.

Fine, A. (2002) *A Shame to Miss*, Books 1, 2 and 3, Corgi Books.

Henri, A. (1989) *Rhinestone Rhino*, Methuen Children's Books.

Ireson, B. (1989) *Rhyme Time*, Beaver Books.

Ireson, B. (1989) *Rhyme Time 2*, Beaver Books.

McGough, R. (1992) *Pillow Talk*, Puffin Books.

Maley, A. (1993) *Short and Sweet 1*, Penguin.

Maley, A. (1995) *Short and Sweet 2*, Penguin.

Maley, A. and Duff, A. (1980) *Variations on a Theme*, CUP.

Orme, D. (1989) *Toughie Toffee*, Lion Books/Collins.

Szkutnik, L. L. (1989) *Lyrics in English*, Warszawa: Wiedza Powszechna.

Source materials for play texts, etc.

Bennett, A. *et al.* (1987) *The Complete Beyond the Fringe*, Methuen.

Berman, E. D. (ed) (1979) *Ten of the Best British Short Plays*, London: Inter-Action Imprint.

Case, D. and Wilson, K. (1979) *Off Stage*, Heinemann.

Case, D. and Wilson, K. (1995a) *English Sketches* (Elementary), Macmillan Heinemann.

Case, D. and Wilson, K. (1995b) *English Sketches* (Intermediate), Macmillan Heinemann.

Dunkling, L. (2000) *Six Sketches*, Penguin.

Durband, A. (ed) (1969) *Playbill One, Two, and Three*, Hutchinson.

Earley, M. and Keil, P. (eds) (1992) *The Classical Monologue: Women*, Methuen Drama.

Earley, M. and Keil, P. (eds) (1992) *The Classical Monologue: Men*, Methuen Drama.

Earley, M. and Keil, P. (eds) (1993) *The Modern Monologue: Women*, Methuen Drama.

Earley, M. and Keil, P. (eds) (1993) *The Modern Monologue: Men*, Methuen Drama.

Earley, M. and Keil, P. (eds) (1995) *The Contemporary Monologue: Women*, Methuen Drama.

Earley, M. and Keil, P. (eds) (1995) *The Contemporary Monologue: Men*, Methuen Drama.

Hampden, J. (ed) (1979) *Twenty-four One-Act Plays*, Edward Arnold.

Hughes, E. (1973) *All is Known*, Evans Bros.

Maley, A. and Duff, A. (1980) *Variations on a Theme*, CUP.

Mankowitz, W. (1956) *Five One-Act Plays*, Evans Bros.

Mortimer, C. (1980) *Dramatic Monologues for Listening Comprehension*, CUP.

Richards, S. (ed) (1978) *Twenty One-Act Plays*, New York: Doubleday.

Shackleton, M. (1985) *Double Act: Ten One-Act Plays on Five Themes*, Edward Arnold.

Schulman, M. and Meckler, E. (1980) *Contemporary Scenes for Student Actors*, New York: Penguin.

The Guide to Selecting Plays for Performance, 91st edition, London: Samuel French.

Watcyn-Jones, P. (1978) *Act English*, Penguin.

Materials on voicework

Berry, C. (1993) *The Actor and the Text*, London: Virgin Books.

Boone, D. R. (1991) *Is Your Voice Telling on You?*, San Diego, California: Singular Publishing Group.

Campbell, D. (1989) *The Roar of Silence: Healing Powers of Breath, Tone and Music*, Wheaton, Illinois: The Theosophical Publishing House.

Chun, S. Tao Cheng (1991) *The Tao of Voice*, Rochester, Vermont: Destiny Books.

McCallion, M. (1988) *The Voice Book*, Faber and Faber.

Maley, A. (2000) *The Language Teacher's Voice*, Macmillan Heinemann.

Martin, S. and Darnley, L. (1996) *The Teaching Voice*, London: Whurr Pubs.

Rodenburg, P. (1998) *The Actor Speaks*, Methuen.

Index

activities format 2–3
adjective + noun phrases 116–17
agreement/disagreement 79–80, 105–6,
124–6, 129–31, 150–1, 154–8, 163
alibis 209–10
'aliens' 120–2
alphabet 11
anticipation 9–10, 15–16, 38, 92–4, 213–16
apology 216–18
appreciation 27, 101, 111
attention (*Notice how ...*) 107–8
auctions 111–12

beliefs 31
body awareness 19–21, 38–9
breathing 18–19, 73–5, 89–92

cartoons 131–4, 231
cause/effect 101, 103, 114–15
certainty 209–10
challenges 209–10
chants 16, 148, 154, 166, 169, 172–4
character 108–11, 114–15, 124–7, 142–4, 232,
236
charades 174–5
chunking 89–94, 166–8
clothing 107–9
comparison 146–7
concentration 9–10, 18–19, 21, 22–3
confidence 13–15, 17–18, 79, 85, 95–6, 230
conflict (scenarios) 216–18
cooperation 9–10, 13–17, 96–8, 175–9
courtroom drama 154–6
cultural differences 7, 120–2, 153–4, 157–9

deduction 114–15
description
of clothing 107–8
of mime 64–5
of objects 45, 99–101, 111–12
of people 39–40, 46–7, 116–17, 123–7,
142–4
of pictures 48–9
of places 39–40, 45–6, 123
of statues 146–7
dialogue 189–98, 202–4, 205–6, 213–16,
222–4
direct speech 200–2
direction (vocab.) 150–1

discussion 3, 190, 230
documentary film scenes 145–6
drama: techniques 2, 240
drama: value 1–2, 229

evaluation (expressions) 57–8, 81–2, 104–5,
168, 170–1, 172–4, 194–8, 202–4,
207–8, 218–24
exaggerated claims 111–12
explanations 136–7, 153–4

feel, smell, taste, touch, etc. 57–8, 161–3
feelings 60, 107, 207–8, 218–20
festivals 153–4
free association 152–3

gesture 166–8
getting to know you 7–8, 26, 47, 166
gobbledy-gook 29, 122, 147–8
greetings 7–8
group bonding 6
non-verbal activities 7–18
verbal exercises 26–8, 29–31, 33–5, 86–7,
96–8, 116–17, 150–1, 169
group formation activities 35–7
group orchestration 85–7, 96–8
group stories 152–3, 170–1

imagination 102–6, 107–8, 113–14, 120–2,
145–58, 207–8
imperatives 150–1, 156–7
improvisation 209–10, 216–18, 234–5
instructions 150–1, 156–7
interest (expressions) 27
interruptions 210–12, 222–4
intonation 24–5, 88–92, 205–8, 224–8,
229–30
inventions 149–50

justifications 123, 153–4, 160–1

laws, legal language 154–6, 157–8
likelihood 114–15, 131–4, 142–4, 163
likes/dislikes 28, 31, 37, 101, 160–1
listening 30, 32–3, 41–3, 83–4, 101, 136–7,
177–9
local environment 45–6
location (vocab.) 38–9, 40, 44–6, 48–9, 123,
136–7, 156–7